WALKING GLYNDŴR'S WAY

WALKING GLYNDŴR'S WAY

A NATIONAL TRAIL THROUGH MID-WALES
by Paddy Dillon

JUNIPER HOUSE, MURLEY MOSS,
OXENHOLME ROAD, KENDAL, CUMBRIA LA9 7RL
www.cicerone.co.uk

© Paddy Dillon 2024
Third edition 2024
ISBN: 978 1 78631 129 0
Second edition 2018
First edition 2014

Printed in Turkey by Pelikan Basim using responsibly sourced paper
A catalogue record for this book is available from the British Library.
All photographs are by the author unless otherwise stated.

© Crown copyright and database rights 2024 OS AC0000810376

Updates to this Guide

While every effort is made by our authors to ensure the accuracy of guidebooks as they go to print, changes can occur during the lifetime of an edition. Any updates that we know of for this guide will be on the Cicerone website (www.cicerone.co.uk/1129/updates), so please check before planning your trip. We also advise that you check information about such things as transport, accommodation and shops locally. Even rights of way can be altered over time. We are always grateful for information about any discrepancies between a guidebook and the facts on the ground, sent by email to updates@cicerone.co.uk.

Register your book: To sign up to receive free updates, special offers and GPX files where available, create a Cicerone account and register your purchase via the 'My Account' tab at www.cicerone.co.uk.

Front cover: Clywedog Reservoir (Day 4)

CONTENTS

Map key 6
Route summary table 7
Overview map with day starts. 8

INTRODUCTION 9
Owain Glyndŵr 10
Geology 14
Landscape 16
Drove roads 17
Wildlife 18
Trees and plants 20
When to walk 21
Getting to and from the route 23
Accommodation 23
Planning your schedule 25
Food and drink 25
Money matters 26
Communications 26
What to pack 27
Waymarking 27
Maps of the route 28
Emergencies 28
Using this guide 28

GLYNDŴR'S WAY 31
Day 1   Knighton to Felindre 32
Day 2   Felindre to Abbeycwmhir 43
Day 3   Abbeycwmhir to Llanidloes 52
Day 4   Llanidloes to Dylife 61
        Ascent of Pen Pumlumon Fawr 72
Day 5   Dylife to Machynlleth 78
Day 6   Machynlleth to Llanbrynmair 88
Day 7   Llanbrynmair to Llanwddyn 98
Day 8   Llanwddyn to Meifod 112
Day 9   Meifod to Welshpool 122

Glyndŵr's Way

Return to Knighton along Offa's Dyke
Day 10   Welshpool to Brompton Cross........................... 131
Day 11   Brompton Cross to Knighton 139

Appendix A   Facilities along the route........................... 150
Appendix B   Pronunciation guide and topographical glossary.......... 153
Appendix C   Useful contacts.................................... 155
Appendix D   Accommodation along the route 157

Route symbols on OS map extracts
(for OS legend see printed OS maps)

- route
- alternative route
- (S) (F) (SF) start, finish and start/finish
- (S) (F) (↑) alternative start, finish and start/finish
- ◄ route direction

GPX files

GPX files for all stages can be downloaded for free at www.cicerone.co.uk/1129/GPX

Features on the overview map

- County/Unitary boundary
- National boundary
- National Park eg **ERYRI**
- Area of Outstanding Natural Beauty eg *Shropshire Hills*

800m / 600m / 400m   200m / 75m / 0m

ROUTE SUMMARY TABLE

11-day schedule as described in this guide

	Start	Finish	Distance	Time	Page
Glyndŵr's Way			**220km (136¾ miles)**		
Day 1	Knighton	Felindre	24.5km (15¼ miles)	8hr	32
Day 2	Felindre	Abbeycwmhir	25km (15½ miles)	8hr	43
Day 3	Abbeycwmhir	Llanidloes	25km (15½ miles)	8hr	52
Day 4	Llanidloes	Dylife	22km (13¾ miles)	6hr 30mins	61
Day 5	Dylife	Machynlleth	25.5km (16 miles)	8hr	78
Day 6	Machynlleth	Llanbrynmair	26km (16 miles)	8hr	88
Day 7	Llanbrynmair	Llanwddyn	29.5km (18½ miles)	9hr	98
Day 8	Llanwddyn	Meifod	24.5km (15¼ miles)	8hr	112
Day 9	Meifod	Welshpool	18km (11 miles)	5hr 30mins	122
Offa's Dyke Path			**47km (29¼ miles)**		
Day 10	Welshpool	Brompton Cross	22.5km (14 miles)	7hr	131
Day 11	Brompton Cross	Knighton	24.5km (15¼ miles)	8hr	139
Route total			**267km (166 miles)**		
Ascent of Pen Pumlumon Fawr (after Day 4)			26km (16 miles)	9hr	72

GLYNDŴR'S WAY

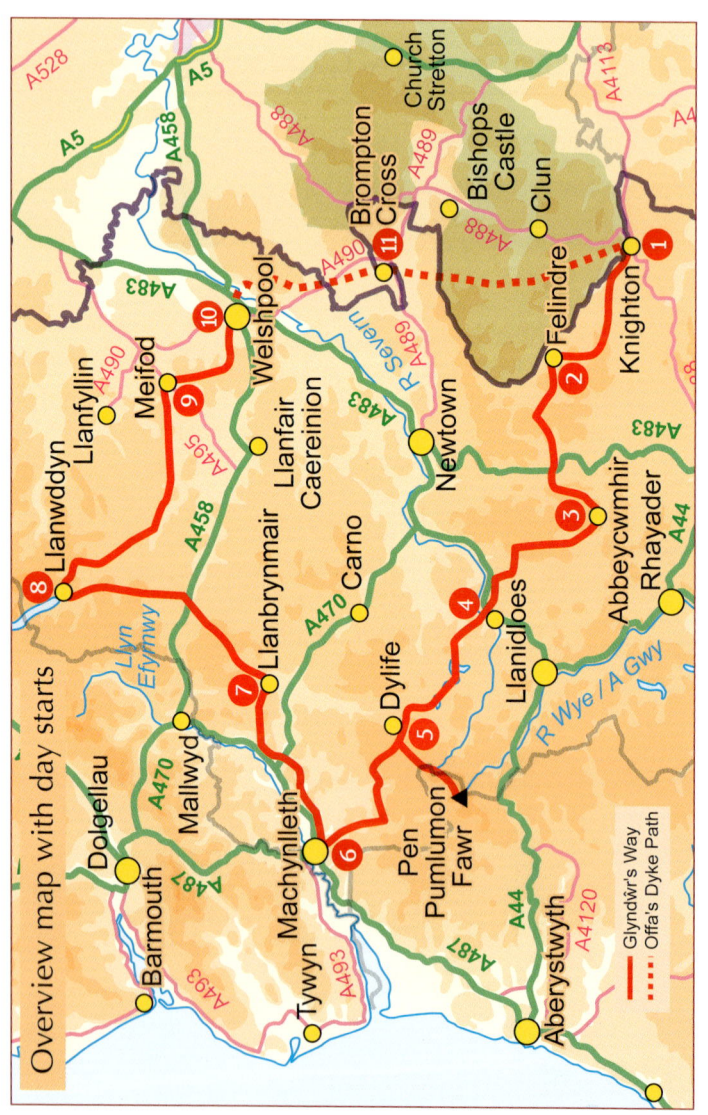

INTRODUCTION

Glyndŵr's Way is named after the remarkable late-medieval Welsh leader Owain Glyndŵr, and is one of three National Trails in Wales. It links at either end – Knighton and Welshpool – with the Offa's Dyke Path, and this guide, as well as describing Glyndŵr's Way, includes two days along the Offa's Dyke Path to create a circular route. The trail is an exploration of the green heart of Wales, chasing the shadow of an inspirational warrior and statesman.

Glyndŵr's Way is one of the quietest National Trails, exploring sparsely populated countryside, featuring a succession of hills and valleys largely used for sheep-rearing. The route meanders around, with frequent twists and turns, ascents and descents, so that the scenery changes continually. Some of the higher parts feature open moorlands or forestry plantations. There are a handful of towns along the way, with a scattering of small villages and abundant small farms. It takes some walkers a long time before they point their feet towards mid-Wales, but once they do so, they always return to experience more of its quiet, understated charm.

Glyndŵr's Way (described in Days 1 to 9 in this guide) sits squarely in mid-Wales, extending almost from

The view from Dyfnant Forest at Pren Croes (Day 7)

'Welcome to Wales' – a notice outside Knighton, the town where Glyndŵr's Way starts

the Wales–England border almost to the coast, a total of 217km (135 miles). It links with the Offa's Dyke Path (Days 10 and 11) to bring walkers back to Knighton, an additional 47km (29 miles), and it links with the Wales Coast Path at its halfway point. The route is entirely confined to the only inland county in Wales – Powys. This county was created in 1974 from three former inland counties – Montgomeryshire, Radnorshire and Brecknockshire. The only towns on Glyndŵr's Way are Knighton, Llanidloes, Machynlleth and Welshpool, but there are also a dozen villages, most of which offer basic services.

OWAIN GLYNDŴR

Any commentary about Owain Glyndŵr quickly becomes a confusing

A stone monument to Owain Glyndŵr, Prince of Wales, in a park at Machynlleth (Day 5)

and contradictory mix of history, myth and legend. There is no doubt that he existed, and that he waged war against English forces. However, it is unlikely that he was gifted with supernatural powers, as was claimed, and no one can say for certain when he died or where he was buried. Like the proverbial old soldier, he just faded away. Shakespeare put boastful words in the mouth of Glendower in *Henry IV, Part I*, while allowing Hotspur a series of caustic put-downs for each utterance, until Mortimer says: 'Come, come, no more of this unprofitable chat.' Not that the other two took much notice of him – they'd barely started!

There are some notable dates and events in Owain Glyndŵr's life, charting his progress from an apparently loyal subject of the Crown to his absolute rejection of English rule and the creation of a Welsh nation-state. The turning point clearly came at a time when Richard II was deposed

OWAIN GLYNDŴR – NOTABLE DATES

- **1354** Possible birth-date of Owain Glyndŵr, descendant of the Princes of Powys. It is known that in later life he spent time with the lawyer David Hanmer and the Earl of Arundel. He also lived in London and studied law.
- **1383** Glyndŵr returned from London to Wales and took residence at Sycharth, where he lived with his wife, sons and daughters.
- **1384** Entered into military service under Richard II, joining a garrison on the Anglo–Scottish border at Berwick-upon-Tweed.
- **1385** Served Richard II on a campaign in Scotland.
- **1386** Called to give evidence at a trial in Chester between Lord Scrope and Sir Robert Grosvenor.
- **1387** Glyndŵr served in Kent against a fleet from Spain, France and Flanders. He returned to Wales afterwards.
- **1390s** Glyndŵr administered his estates and had complimentary lines composed about him by the bard Iolo Goch. However, Lord Grey appropriated land belonging to Glyndŵr, and despite appeals to the King and Parliament the land was never returned. In fact, Glyndŵr and the Welsh in general were insulted during this dispute.
- **1399** Richard II was deposed, and Henry IV was crowned King of England.
- **1400** Lord Grey informed Glyndŵr too late about a requirement to send troops to serve in Scotland, apparently so that Glyndŵr could be called a traitor. This led to the beginnings of a revolt and skirmishes around

Wales, and later in the year Glyndŵr declared himself Prince of Wales at Glyndyfrdwy.

- **1401** The revolt spread throughout most of northern and central Wales, with the Welsh capturing Conwy Castle. An amnesty was offered by Henry Percy (Hotspur) to restore order, but this was not extended to Glyndŵr or the cousins who aided his campaign. Glyndŵr scored a notable victory over an English force at Hyddgen on Pumlumon.
- **1402** The English enacted anti-Welsh legislation, which encouraged more Welsh support for Glyndŵr. Lord Grey and Sir Edmund Mortimer were captured by the Welsh – the latter at the Battle of Pilleth. Henry IV paid a ransom for Grey, but refused to pay for Mortimer, so Mortimer later entered into an alliance with Glyndŵr. There was also a measure of French military support for Wales.
- **1403** The revolt gathered pace, with Welsh scholars and labourers leaving England and returning to Wales to assist Glyndŵr's campaign. Some Welshmen serving in the English army also abandoned their posts and returned to Wales to fight alongside their countrymen. Hotspur switched allegiance and was slain by the King's men. By the end of the year, Glyndŵr was in control of most of Wales.
- **1404** Glyndŵr assembled his Parliament at Machynlleth, where the bold 'Tripartite Indenture' was drawn up. This proposed a territorial division in which Glyndŵr would control Wales, Mortimer would control the south and west of England, while Percy, Earl of Northumberland, would control the midlands and north of England. Glyndŵr's power remained strong throughout Wales.

A stone tablet on Owain Glyndŵr's Parliament House in the centre of Machynlleth

- **1405** This was known as 'The Year of the French' in Wales. A treaty had been negotiated between Wales and France. A French force landed at Milford Haven and marched across country to within 8 miles of Worcester, only to retire after an indecisive stand-off with the English army.
- **1406** Glyndŵr wrote to Charles VI of France, in a document known as 'The Pennal Letter', offering to transfer Church control in Wales from Rome to Avignon in return for military support. This was not

The monumental Clock Tower in the centre of Knighton, where Glyndŵr's Way begins

forthcoming. Meanwhile, the English pushed through Anglesey and gradually assumed control of the whole island, as well as strengthening other positions around Wales.
- **1407** The English, rather than engaging in outright conflict, deployed their forces to cut supply lines to Glyndŵr and his followers. Aberystwyth Castle was captured, along with some of Glyndŵr's family members.
- **1408** Glyndŵr once again became a fugitive guerrilla leader, aided by his remaining supporters, who were dwindling in number.
- **1409** Edmund Mortimer died during the siege of Harlech Castle.
- **1410** Harlech Castle was captured by English forces. Glyndŵr mounted a bloody incursion into Shropshire, but some of his leading supporters were captured.
- **1412** Glyndŵr's last definite engagement – an ambush in Brecon. After this, no one knows for certain what became of him.
- **1413** Henry IV died and was succeeded by Henry V. Royal pardons were offered to Welsh rebel leaders, but nothing was heard from Glyndŵr. It has been suggested that he became a monk, or lived out his years with one of his daughters, or simply died on the hills. Some say he never died at all!
- **2003–4** A large online poll resulted in Owain Glyndŵr being ranked in second place on a list of '100 Welsh Heroes'. In first and third place, respectively, were politician Aneurin Bevan and singer Tom Jones!
- **2015** The 600th anniversary of the assumed death of Owain Glyndŵr.

and Henry IV was crowned King of England.

GEOLOGY

The geology of mid-Wales dates largely from the Ordovician and Silurian periods, some 485–420 million years ago. At that time, 'Wales' and 'England' were a shallow sea off the continent of Avalonia. 'Scotland' and 'Northern Ireland' were far away, across the deep-water Iapetus Ocean, on the continent of Laurentia. As the continents were being worn down by the weather, vast quantities of mud, sand and gravel were washed into the sea by powerful rivers. The sediments spread through the shallow sea into the deeper ocean, settling to form thick beds that became compressed into hard rocks.

There were volcanic episodes, represented by rocks found around Builth Wells and Welshpool, which pushed into existing rock beds and deformed them. They include dolerite intrusions and basaltic lava flows.

During the Devonian period, the rock beds in the oceanic basin were crumpled together, folded into vast arches and troughs. The sea receded and mountains were pushed up in its place. Some of the mudstones became compressed into slates, later useful for construction, while other rocks simply sheared and crumbled, and these proved quite useless for building.

On many parts of Glyndŵr's Way, the rock is buried out of sight, but farm tracks are occasionally worn to bedrock, and the layers of rock are seen tilted anywhere between 45° and vertical. Watch out for roadside rock cuttings or small quarries, as natural rock outcrops are scarce along the route.

An extensive ore-field was created through hydro-thermal activity in the Permian period, around 300 million years ago. The ore-field was mined chiefly for lead and copper, but also provided zinc and a little silver, while 'waste' minerals such as barytes were later reclaimed, once uses were discovered for them.

You have to look elsewhere around Wales to find significantly younger rock types. However, other changes have taken place in the landscape. Within the past two million years, the hills of mid-Wales were completely glaciated and scoured to bedrock. Glaciers carved deep valleys, then melt-water ensured that they were filled with ill-assorted rubble and sediments, and occasional lakes. Over the past 10,000 years, vegetation and life crept back into

Some of the rock in mid-Wales is remarkably strong and durable, making good building material

GLYNDŴR'S WAY

the region, which has since been adapted and shaped by a few thousand years of human settlement, agriculture and industry.

LANDSCAPE

The overwhelming impression of mid-Wales is of intensively sheep-grazed grassy hills, with rather unmemorable profiles, separated by verdant valleys and occasional moorlands. The landscape is surprisingly well settled and agricultural, with many farmsteads dotted around. However, there are only a handful of small towns and a few tiny villages, linked by a network of meandering minor roads, a small number of main roads, and even fewer railways. On some elevated areas, views in all directions suggest there are no habitations at all, but there will often be a farm or a house tucked into a nearby hollow.

Some poor-quality agricultural land has been turned over to forestry, and some forests are quite extensive. Plantations developed 50 years ago have often been harvested and replanted. Some windswept moorlands have caught the attention of 'wind farm' developers, and there are a handful of extensive upland sites featuring dozens of whirling wind turbines. As such developments have been banned in the Eryri (Snowdonia)

Most of the ancient bedrock in mid-Wales is friable and breaks down into small stones

Land use in the hills of mid-Wales includes sheep-rearing, forestry and upland wind farms

and Bannau Brycheiniog (Brecon Beacons) national parks, they have become concentrated in the hills of mid-Wales. The power companies have plans to expand, but there are considerable local lobbies against them.

DROVE ROADS

Cattle and other livestock have been driven across country for centuries, but with the steady growth of towns and cities in England in the 18th and 19th centuries, the need for fresh meat to be delivered to markets resulted in large cattle droves. Great herds of Welsh cattle would be marched hundreds of miles to markets. Specially bred corgi dogs would snap at their heels to keep them on course, while being small enough to avoid the inevitable kick! Drovers had to be tough, hard-working and honest. In fact, when the trade became subject to regulation and licensing, drovers had to be married men and householders, aged over 30.

Drovers had to be very good at handling money and negotiations, so they were often trusted to carry important messages and documents, and to settle debts between people. If someone in Wales needed to pay a debt in London or Birmingham, he could entrust the money to a drover, who would probably leave it at home. On arrival in the city, he could sell his cattle, settle the other person's debts out of the proceeds, and not have to risk robbery by carrying money back to Wales. Drovers founded the Black Ox Bank in Llandovery, which existed for two centuries before being acquired by Lloyds Bank.

Drovers would often find themselves in conflict with people whose property they passed, so they were adept at defending themselves. It was often easier for other people to keep their own cattle away from those of the drovers, and to suffer any damage to fences in silence, repairing them once the drovers had passed. Wealthy drovers would frequent inns and taverns, while less affluent drovers would pitch overnight camps for themselves.

While some drovers were willing to pay tolls to use turnpike roads, enabling them to reach their markets faster, others avoided tolls by taking longer and more arduous journeys across country. Some would even face down toll collectors, refusing to pay! Droving was brought to a standstill in the mid-19th century, when railways offered faster and more efficient transport. Some old drove roads became part of the regular road network, but vestiges of old drove roads can still be distinguished over the hills of mid-Wales. They usually have their boundary fences, walls or hedges a considerable distance apart. A number of old drove roads are used on Glyndŵr's Way, but today's walkers have to make an effort to imagine what they were like in their heyday.

WILDLIFE

It is necessary to watch carefully to spot wildlife in mid-Wales. There is so much domestic stock, in the shape of countless sheep, rather fewer cattle,

The concrete dam of the Clywedog Reservoir (Day 4)

Semi-wild ponies are occasionally seen grazing on some uplands in mid-Wales

and a few horses, that the wildlife almost goes unnoticed. There are deer, and the easiest to spot are the fallow deer that graze near Powis Castle. Other large mammals include semi-wild ponies, as well as foxes, badgers and hares, although these are seldom seen. Rabbits are numerous in some places, but virtually absent in others. Among the rarest mammals of all are pine martens.

Primarily, this is bird-watching country, and walkers with their eyes to the skies will be richly rewarded. Mid-Wales is often referred to as 'Kite Country'. Red kites were persecuted around Britain until they were left clinging for survival in one small part of mid-Wales. Given assistance in the form of feeding stations, as well as legal protection, they are now commonly seen quartering the skies, along with buzzards, hen harriers, merlins and peregrines. Towards the coast, near Machynlleth, ospreys can also be spotted in the summer.

On elevated moorlands, watch for red grouse, curlew, snipe and hen harrier, along with smaller birds such as skylark, meadow pipit, ring ouzel, wheatear and whinchat. Moorland pools will attract a number of waders and wildfowl in the autumn and winter, including golden plover, sandpiper, tufted duck and goldeneye. Rivers may be frequented by the small, dark brown dipper, with its white bib, which uses its wings to swim underwater. Commercial forestry plantations attract crossbills, whose curious beaks enable them to extract pine seeds from pinecones.

There are a couple of notable nature reserves along Glyndŵr's

GLYNDŴR'S WAY

Way, managed by the Radnorshire and Montgomery Wildlife Trusts. For more information check with the Radnorshire Wildlife Trust (www.rwtwales.org), Montgomery Wildlife Trust (www.montwt.co.uk) and Dyfi Osprey Project (www.dyfiospreyproject.com). The RSPB operate a visitor centre and bird hides at Lake Vyrnwy (www.rspb.org.uk).

TREES AND PLANTS

The original wildwoods of mid-Wales have long been cleared, and any deciduous woodlands remaining are likely to be secondary plantations. Common native trees include oak, ash and birch, with willow and alder more likely to favour wetter ground. Stout horse chestnut and sycamore are often present, while holly forms a common understorey. Some woodlands are undoubtedly centuries old, with splendid ground cover including lush bluebells and garlic-scented ramsons. In many places where building stone was in short supply for walls, trees were pressed into service to make hedgerows – including hawthorn, blackthorn and hazel. Some hedgerows are still trimmed, but others have been allowed to grow rampant. Sometimes, the only remains of long-forgotten hedgerows are widely spaced tall trees, stretching ahead in a long line through fields.

Commercial forestry plantations appear from time to time along

Glyndŵr's Way crosses a wooded ravine between Moelfre and Newchapel (Day 3)

WHEN TO WALK

Bluebells are a common sight in spring in many of the longer-established woodlands in mid-Wales

Glyndŵr's Way, generally featuring imported firs and spruces. However, even in these forests the margins of the plantations, spared from sheep grazing, often sprout self-seeded trees such as birch, willow and rowan. Some long-established parklands, especially near the small towns along the route, occasionally feature exceptionally tall and stout specimen trees, even including giant redwoods.

Given the extensive nature of sheep-grazing in the hills of mid-Wales, grassy fields often struggle to produce flowers, although some meadows reserved for mowing may produce a blaze of buttercups and dandelions. One of the most cheerful flowers seen in mid-Wales is the yellow 'Welsh' poppy. Primroses often provide an early splash of pale yellow, while foxgloves and heather make roadsides and moorlands blush purple in summer. Brambles are often tangled among hedgerows, producing white blossom in summer, then blackberries in autumn. On moorlands, bilberries and crowberries fruit in autumn.

The greatest range of flowering plants are likely to be seen tangled in hedgerows and along roadside verges and riversides, where they cannot be mown or grazed. Often steep slopes and marginal land are covered with invasive bracken or dense gorse bushes that blaze with yellow, coconut-scented flowers.

WHEN TO WALK

Glyndŵr's Way could be walked at almost any time of year, but there have been times, such as the winter/spring of 2012–13, when excessively deep, long-lying snow made it almost impossible to walk many parts of the route.

Most walkers will aim for summertime in the hope of warm, sunny days and not too much rain. This is also a colourful time to walk, with plenty of flowers and blossom during May and June, with trees coming into full leaf, followed by a flush of purple heather on the higher moors in August.

Bear in mind that some short stretches cross permanently boggy ground, and after prolonged rain some paths and tracks become quite muddy. It is well worth checking

The ruins of the Bryntail Lead Mine can be explored below the dam of the Clywedog Reservoir (Day 4)

daily weather forecasts during your walk.

GETTING TO AND FROM THE ROUTE

By train
The terminal points of Glyndŵr's Way (Knighton and Welshpool) are served by two railway lines fanning out from Shrewsbury, which is itself easily accessed from mainline rail services through Birmingham. Transport for Wales trains run along the Heart of Wales Line between Shrewsbury and Swansea, serving Knighton around half a dozen times per day in both directions, but only once or twice on Sundays. Transport for Wales trains run along the Cambrian Line between Shrewsbury, Welshpool and Machynlleth, around a dozen times per day in both directions, with slightly less on Sundays. Transport for Wales trains also reach Machynlleth from Aberystwyth and Pwllheli. Full timetable details can be checked at tfw.wales. See also Appendix C.

By bus
Bus services are patchy around the course of Glyndŵr's Way, being fairly regular and frequent in and near towns, and completely absent in some other areas. It is possible to walk for three days without intercepting a single bus route. The towns of Knighton, Llanidloes, Machynlleth and Welshpool offer the greatest range of services, although some bus connections might need to be made off-route in towns such as Newtown. See Appendix C.

The only useful bus service on a single stage of Glyndŵr's Way is the one linking Machynlleth, Cemmaes Road and Llanbrynmair, which runs daily, except Sundays. Full details of bus services around Powys and Glyndŵr's Way can be checked on www.traveline.cymru.

ACCOMMODATION

There are several hotels, guesthouses and B&Bs in the towns along Glyndŵr's Way, but these can become fully booked on summer weekends, or whenever there is a local festival or wedding. In the smaller villages, there might only be a couple of lodgings, and if these are already full it could be half a day's walk to the next available place.

The best approach is to have flexible dates for your trek, then start contacting places where you want to stay. If you reach an impasse at one point, then check whether an alternative day is free and rework the rest of your schedule. In some instances, there may be a bus service to a nearby place, or an off-route accommodation provider might be willing to offer a pick-up and drop-off service. There are walking holiday companies who can book all your

Campsites are available at intervals along Glyndŵr's Way

accommodation and arrange baggage transfer (see Appendix C) – for a price.

For a summary of the types of accommodation available on or near Glyndŵr's Way and the route back to Knighton see Appendix A. For a selection of accommodation providers along the whole route see Appendix D. For a more comprehensive and up-to-date list, along the route from Knighton to Welshpool, visit the Glyndŵr's Way page on the National Trails website (www.nationaltrail.co.uk/en_GB/trails/glyndwrs-way).

Some wayfarers prefer to camp, and there is a fairly good spread of campsites along the route (see Appendix A). These occur almost at daily intervals, with some intermediate sites. A full list of campsites, and occasional bunkhouses, is available on the website www.nationaltrail.co.uk/en_GB/trails/glyndwrs-way.

Occasionally, a campsite might need to be pre-booked, or facilities might be quite basic, so it is worth checking these in advance. Wild camping opportunities are quite limited, as so much of the countryside is agricultural, and the rest is often forested or rugged, boggy moorland. Anyone wishing to camp wild should ask permission of the landowner, but in many cases it will be hard to find out who this is.

PLANNING YOUR SCHEDULE

For efficient arrival and departure, try to avoid travelling by public transport on Sundays, unless there are services that really do suit you. Even so, careful study of timetables is recommended (see Appendix C for more information on public transport). Once you know when you can start walking, you can plan where you are going to stay. Most experienced walkers are capable of covering around 24km (15 miles) a day, and Glyndŵr's Way naturally breaks into stages of approximately that length (along with an optional ascent of Pumlumon Fawr after Day 4). This is what is described in this guide.

If this proves too far in a day, then there are often opportunities to break mid-way through each day. However, bear in mind that not all mid-way points feature accommodation.

See the route summary table and the facilities table (Appendix A) to help you plan your route.

In a sense, there aren't really 'hard' or 'easy' days on the trail. Every day includes a number of hills, and ascents and descents may occasionally be steep, but are usually reasonably gentle. Most of the surfaces underfoot are firm and clear, including tracks and minor roads, but sometimes there are pathless fields or occasional boggy moorland paths. The fact that the terrain changes all the time means that some stretches can be covered quickly, while others prove slower, but overall each stage is likely to take the same amount of time.

Most accommodation providers will ask when you are likely to arrive, and it is usually a good idea to quote a time period of at least an hour either side of when you guess you might arrive. If anything prevents you arriving on time, let your host know, so that they aren't unduly worried and don't call out the emergency services unnecessarily.

Public transport is of limited help to the walker doing the route in sections. The only options would be to organise pick-ups or call for taxis.

FOOD AND DRINK

There are daily opportunities to pick up food and drink along Glyndŵr's Way, but in some places there are plenty of options, while in other places there is very little (see Appendix A). Opening times of pubs, restaurants, cafés and shops vary widely. Some accommodation providers offer evening meals and packed lunches, while others don't. In areas where food and drink is sparse, it is worth bearing in mind what is actually available, as well as checking opening times. If there is a chance that places will be closed, then you will need to buy supplies in advance and carry them for one or two stages.

Full details of all pubs, restaurants, cafés and shops along

The Cann Office Hotel offers food, drink and accommodation in the village of Llangadfan

Glyndŵr's Way can be checked on the website www.nationaltrail.co.uk/en_GB/trails/glyndwrs-way.

MONEY MATTERS

Banking services have been drastically reduced in recent years and post offices often have very limited business hours. Obtaining cash on a daily basis isn't possible, and in some places cashpoints might only be available in supermarkets. Be sure to carry sufficient cash as not all businesses are able to deal with credit/debit cards.

COMMUNICATIONS

Rural telephone kiosks are quickly vanishing; they seldom accept coins, and have to be operated by entering credit/debit card details or an account number. Mobile phone coverage is patchy around mid-Wales, and signals come and go at odd times. The towns have good coverage, but some villages have no signal, and being on high ground is no guarantee that a signal will be available. If being in contact by mobile phone is important to you, then keep an eye on signal strength as you walk. Some accommodation providers offer internet/wi-fi.

There are post offices in all the towns along the route, as well as in a few of the little villages. Usually, they are post office shops. Opening times may be quite limited in the villages, and they won't provide the full range of services that an office in town provides. Post is generally collected daily, except Sundays, and will generally leave mid-Wales promptly for its destination.

WHAT TO PACK

If you want to travel lightweight, there are walking holiday companies who can transfer baggage from place to place around the trail. However, as conditions in hilly mid-Wales aren't much different to most other hilly parts of Britain, it is essential that all walkers carry with them warm and waterproof clothing, especially if travelling early or late in the year. Some cooler clothing, a sunhat and sunscreen might be more appropriate if blessed with sunny summer weather. Walking poles are a matter of personal preference, as is footwear. However, bear in mind that some parts can be wet and boggy throughout the year, and some paths and tracks get very muddy after prolonged rain. Spare casual clothing for the evenings is useful, as it can be worn whenever the walking clothes need to be washed.

Unless food and drink can be guaranteed around lunchtime, carry a packed lunch and drink. Water from streams along Glyndŵr's Way is not guaranteed to be clean, as it often runs through sheep or cattle pastures, or through farmyards. Unless you are prepared to filter, treat or boil water, you should carry enough clean water for each day's needs.

If camping, a lightweight tent, sleeping bag and cooking equipment will be sufficient. Most campsites along the way are low level and sheltered.

WAYMARKING

Waymarking along Glyndŵr's Way is often very good and nearly always more than adequate. Only rarely is it necessary to watch more carefully than usual for signposts and marker posts. However, it only needs one marker at a crucial turning to go missing, and it could leave wayfarers floundering, so keep an eye on the map and the written route description.

Glyndŵr's Way is unique among the National Trails in that it features two completely different types of marker. The standard National Trail acorn marker is used, but in almost every instance a two-legged red dragon symbol is also used. Every signpost and marker post also includes a directional marker. In some places, this will simply point straight ahead, but in other places, left and right turnings may come in rapid succession. On some occasions, marker posts might also include directional arrows for adjoining public rights of way, so watch carefully when arrows point in all directions.

GLYNDŴR'S WAY

Glyndŵr's Way marker posts, old and new

MAPS OF THE ROUTE

The maps in this guidebook are extracted from the Ordnance Survey 1:50,000 Landranger series. They show the route and some of the land either side of it. If you wish to see more of the terrain through which the route passes, then you will need the following Landranger maps – 125, 126, 135, 136 and 137. For more detail, use the following Ordnance Survey 1:25,000 Explorer maps – 200, 201, 214, 215, 216 and 239. If you wish to include the additional two days of walking along the Offa's Dyke Path, or the ascent of Pen Pumlumon Fawr, these maps also cover those options.

EMERGENCIES

In case of emergency, the police, ambulance, fire service or mountain rescue can be alerted by dialling 999 or the European emergency number 112. Be ready to give full details about the nature of the emergency, and ensure that you are able to keep in touch with the responders, who may request further information from you.

USING THIS GUIDE

In this guide Glyndŵr's Way is divided into nine day stages, starting at Knighton and ending at Welshpool. These stages average about 24km (15

A track runs down from Upper Esgair Hill to a tiny settlement called Bwlch-y-sarnau (Day 3)

miles) in length, and each one finishes in a place with accommodation available at the end of the day. There are often opportunities to break mid-way through each day, but not all mid-way points feature accommodation. After Day 4 there is an optional ascent of Pumlumon Fawr, which will require an extra day. Days 10 and 11 follow the Offa's Dyke Path to return walkers to Knighton.

The guide describes each day's walk along the route, and key information (such as distance, time, refreshment and transport links) is provided in a box at the beginning of the route description. Note that the figure given for 'time' is for walking only, and doesn't include stops for lunch or any other breaks.

To aid navigation, significant places and features along the way that appear on the OS map are shown in **bold** in the route description. Information on places of interest en route is also provided.

A table of facilities available along the route at the time of going to press appears in Appendix A. Appendix B is a glossary of topographical terms and a guide to Welsh pronunciation. Appendix C provides a list of useful contacts in case you need further information.

Approaching Foel Fadian – the highest point reached on Glyndŵr's Way (Day 5)

GPX tracks

GPX tracks for the stages in this guidebook are available to download free at www.cicerone.co.uk/1129/GPX. If you have not bought the book through the Cicerone website, or have bought the book without opening an account, please register your purchase in your Cicerone library to access GPX and update information.

A GPS device is an excellent aid to navigation, but you should also carry a map and compass and know how to use them. GPX files are provided in good faith, but in view of the profusion of formats and devices, neither the author nor the publisher accepts responsibility for their use. We provide files in a single standard GPX format that works on most devices and systems, but you may need to convert files to your preferred format using a GPX converter such as gpsvisualizer.com or one of the many other apps and online converters available.

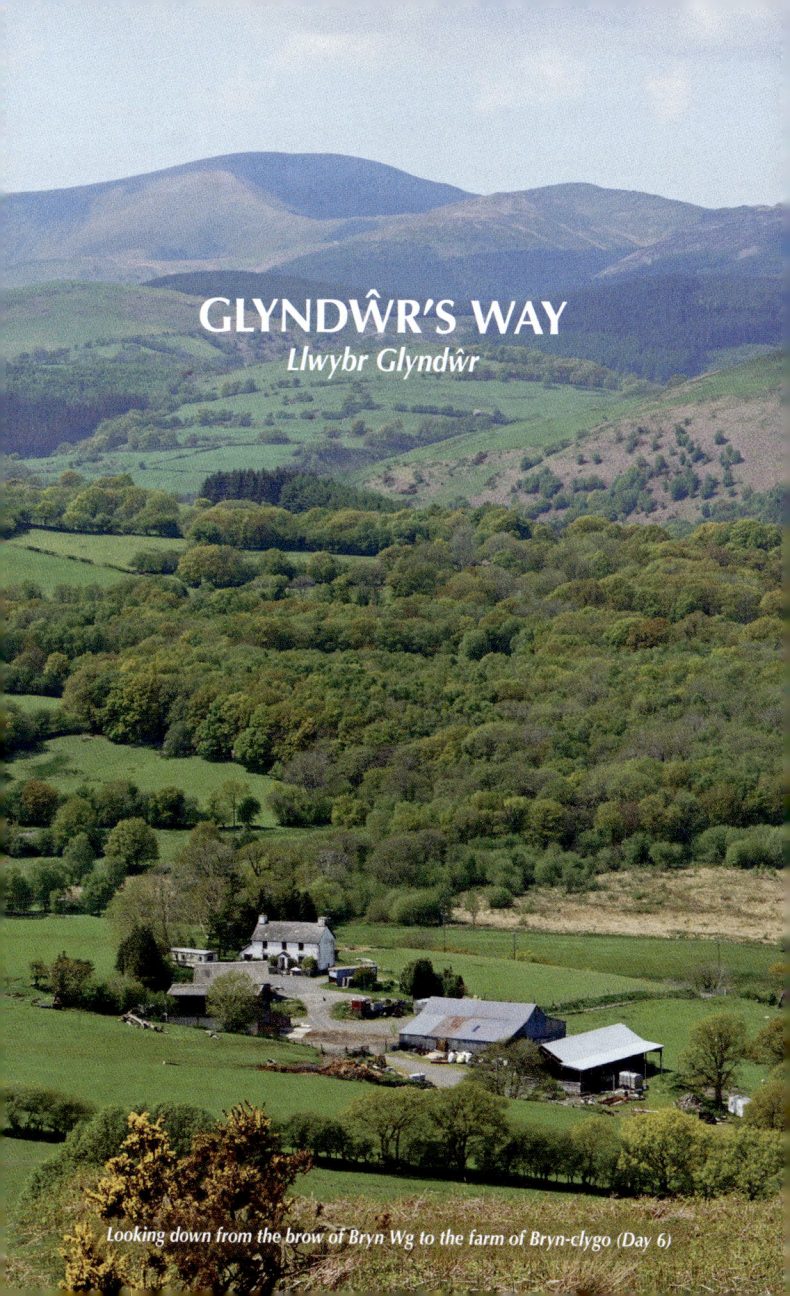

GLYNDŴR'S WAY
Llwybr Glyndŵr

Looking down from the brow of Bryn Wg to the farm of Bryn-clygo (Day 6)

DAY 1
Knighton to Felindre

Start	Clock Tower, Knighton
Finish	Wharf Inn, Felindre
Distance	24.5km (15¼ miles)
Ascent	695m (2280ft)
Descent	610m (2000ft)
Time	8hr
Terrain	Valleys, farmland and hill pastures, followed by high, open moorland
Maps	OS Landranger 136, 137
Refreshment	Plenty of choice in Knighton. Greyhound Inn at Llangunllo. Wharf Inn at Felindre.
Transport	Knighton and Llangunllo are served by trains from Shrewsbury and Swansea

Glyndŵr's Way quickly leaves Knighton, crossing Bailey Hill to reach the little village of Llangunllo. Walkers who leave Knighton around midday should consider staying overnight near Llangunllo, or catch a train back to Knighton. Those who start early will have plenty of time to continue over the sprawling moorlands of Pool Hill, Stanky Hill and Black Mountain. Bear in mind that accommodation is very limited in the villages, and if relying on pub grub in the evening, it is wise to check at the planning stage that the pubs will be open.

KNIGHTON

The small market town of Knighton, with a charter granted in 1230, is also known as Tref-y-Clawdd ('town on the dyke'). The dyke referred to is the eighth-century Offa's Dyke, which passes straight through the centre of the town, and some of its finest stretches run over nearby hills. There are also the remains of two Norman motte and baileys – one of them marked on the map as Bryn-y-Castell, and the other located at the highest point in town, on private land. The higher castle was destroyed by Owain Glyndŵr in 1402. The bulk of Knighton is in Wales, but

DAY 1 – KNIGHTON TO FELINDRE

a few buildings on the northern side of the River Teme lie in England, making this a true border (or 'Marches') town. Anyone able to spare the time to explore should start at the Offa's Dyke Centre, which provides lots of local information, as well as commentaries about Owain Glyndŵr and Glyndŵr's Way (tel 01547 528753).

Knighton is served by the Heart of Wales line, which runs between Shrewsbury and Swansea, featuring splendid scenery for the most part. The town offers a fine range of services, including hotels, B&Bs and a nearby campsite, as well as plenty of shops, pubs, restaurants, cafés and takeaways. There is a post office, bank with ATM, local bus services and taxis. The next place with a similar range of services, Llanidloes, is three days ahead along the trail.

Glyndŵr's Way marker stones on the steep High Street, also appropriately known as The Narrows

In 1402, south of Knighton, Owain Glyndŵr divided his small force of Welshmen and successfully engaged a larger English force led by Edmund Mortimer. During the **Battle of Pilleth**, or Bryn Glas, it is said that a number of Welsh archers serving under Mortimer suddenly switched sides. The field was strewn with bodies that lay unburied until they reeked, and some accounts accuse Welsh women of mutilating the corpses. Eventually, the remains were piled into a mass grave, now marked by a stand of tall Wellingtonias, beside St Mary's Church at Pilleth. Mortimer was captured and held in Machynlleth.

Start at the top of Broad Street in the centre of **Knighton**, where the monumental Clock Tower has stood since 1872, around 185m (610ft). There is a signpost for Llangunllo. Climb straight up High Street, appropriately known as The Narrows, which is steep, pedestrianised and narrow, passing ornamental marker stones for Glyndŵr's Way. ◄ At the top of the street, beside The Golden Lion, turn left along Castle Road, then turn right downhill. The road narrows and is barred to traffic.

Cross another road and continue down a tarmac path. Turn right along a back street at Cross Cottage. This narrows, becoming a tarmac path running alongside a river, and continues along another back street, reaching a narrow road at Mill Lodge. Cross this road and walk up a narrow tarmac path as signposted. Continue up to a road at Green Acre, in the suburb of **Garth**. Cross the road, slightly to the left, to pick up another signposted path. This is narrow and grassy, flanked by hedgerows and fences, climbing to a road bend at Rock House. Turn right down the road, then quickly left as signposted, past Ivy Cottage. Follow a grassy track where there are plenty of trees alongside, but not enough to block views of Knighton.

Go through a gate onto the wooded slopes of **Garth Hill** and walk down a path with a wooden edge. Keep straight ahead as marked at junctions, and the path later rises without a wooden edge. Later, go through a gate to continue with a fence alongside. When the path leaves the woods, it becomes a grassy track flanked by hedges, rising to join a minor road. Turn left, in effect straight ahead, to follow the road up to a triangular junction. Turn left as signposted for Knighton, and keep straight ahead downhill at a nearby junction.

Note the acorn and dragon waymarker symbols, repeated hundreds of times throughout the walk.

Day 1 – Knighton to Felindre

Turn right at another triangular road junction and climb past the farm of Little Cwm-gilla. The road climbs steeply and the tarmac ends at Ebrandy Cottage. Continue straight ahead up a track flanked by hedges, often with deep ruts worn by tractor tyres, with views back towards Knighton. Reach a gate beside a small plantation on a hill top at 393m (1290ft). The track swings right and expires, so walk straight ahead instead, through a gate, and follow a hedgerow onwards, which leads down into a dip.

After passing a gate, a muddy track climbs from a small pond to a junction. Turn left and continue uphill. A hedge to the left is trimmed hawthorn, while to the right are peculiarly shaped hawthorn trees that formed a 'laid' hedge many decades ago, but now grow tall. Go through gates used as a sheepfold, around 410m (1345ft), near the top of **Bailey Hill**. Continue across high fields with hardly any sight of habitation – just rolling hills and valleys. A gentle descent leads through a gate, and a further descent leads to a junction with gates. Simply walk straight ahead as signposted for Llangunllo. Go down a grassy track, down beside a field and through a gate. The path is grassy, flanked by gorse bushes, and runs parallel

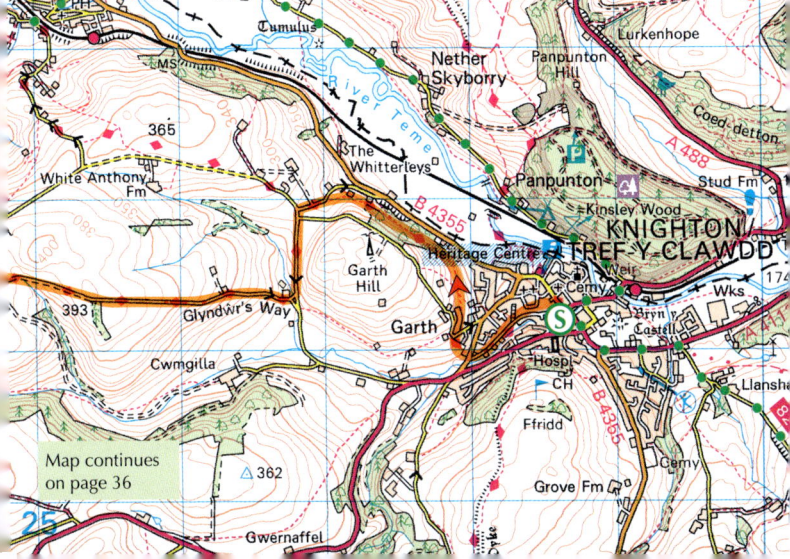

to a motor-rally track. This is the Phil Price Rally School course (www.philprice.co.uk), and it could be very noisy and dusty when in use.

Turn left through a gate and walk down through a field, crossing a stream as marked. Walk up a broad field path, then turn right as signposted, down through a gate as marked. Continue down through a field, reaching the bottom corner, and go through another gate. Turn right down a track, which immediately bends left. Pass near a fishpond and walk up to a junction. Keep left and walk down through a track intersection, straight past a notice-board explaining about **Cefnsuran Farm**.

Cefnsuran Farm covers about 120 hectares (300 acres) and is predominantly for rearing sheep, where Welsh Mule ewes are put to Texel, Bleu du Maine and Suffolk rams. There are also Charolais cross cattle and a few working ponies. Self-catering accommodation is available, and the Rally School is close to hand.

The Greyhound Inn sits at a crossroads in the village of Llangunllo

Don't head left towards the farm, but watch for a gap between trees, where there is a marker post. Walk up through the trees a short way and go through a small gate, then turn left up a track into a farmyard. Turn right to leave it, going through a gate and following a track uphill. This runs through two more gates as it climbs through fields, then it expires. Climb straight to the top of a field and go through a small gate beside a tall tree. Veer slightly right through the next field, and go down through a small gate onto a narrow road.

Turn left down the road a short way, watching for another small gate on the right. This leads onto a path dropping from the road, down through woods, and crossing a track. Go through a gate and continue down through fields, following the path between houses at Lugg View, to join the **B4356** road. Turn right along the road, crossing the River Lugg to enter **Llangunllo**, around 230m (755ft).

Leave the village by walking down the road signposted for the station. Cross the **River Lugg**, then walk uphill and eventually pass straight through a crossroads.

GLYNDŴR'S WAY

LLANGUNLLO

St Cynllo is said to have lived in a monastic cell in this area in the fifth or sixth century, and the church bearing his name is thought to date from the 13th century. The current building is a 19th-century 'restoration', but it incorporates features that may date from the 14th century.

The Greyhound Inn sits on a central crossroads and served as both pub and community shop until 2006. It closed for a while following the death of 92-year-old Bill Matheson, thought to be one of the longest-serving landlords in Wales, with 45 years spent pulling pints. Distraught villagers were reduced to using the bus shelter across the road as an impromptu bar! The inn reopened, although there is no longer a shop in the village, despite the old-fashioned shop signs attached to one building. There is a B&B outside the village at Rhiwlas, at Llancoch.

Llangunllo is connected by rail to Knighton, Shrewsbury and Swansea, although the railway halt is 2km (1¼ miles) distant.

When the road bends right, keep straight ahead through a gate and go down a grassy path. Cross a footbridge and climb, keeping right to follow a hedge alongside the top of a field, to reach a gate and a road bend. Turn right to follow the road, which quickly runs beneath a railway bridge. ◄ Turn left immediately up a farm access track, keeping left of a house called Nayadd Fach. Go up through a gate and pass a stand of conifers, still climbing. The track changes from stony to grassy and goes through another gate. Continue almost to a farm building, but turn left beforehand, through yet another gate as marked.

The railway station is about 600 metres further along the road.

Turn right to follow a fence and hedge onwards, beside a field. Turn right through a gate and cross a little footbridge, then quickly turn left through another gate as marked. Immediately bear right and follow a path rising through the middle of the field, to the top, and go through

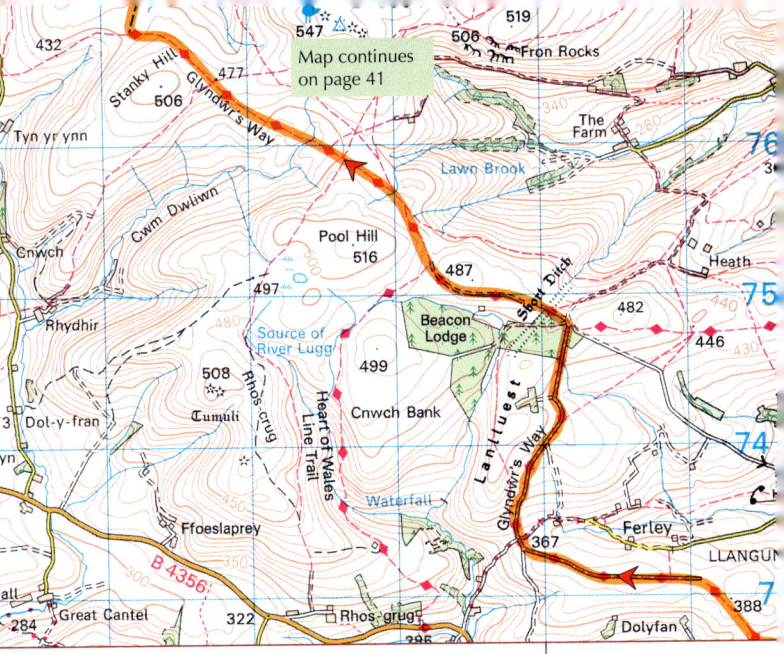

yet another gate. Walk gently downhill, with a fence to the right, through a gate into another field, then over a slight rise to a final gate. Join and follow a grassy track flanked by fences, rising gently above **Ferley**, over 380m (1245ft).

The track later falls to a junction with a gravel track. Turn right to follow it across a dip at 367m (1205ft), then climb. ▶ Apart from another dip along the way, the track climbs and briefly enters a forest, leaving it at a gate and junction around 460m (1510ft). Turn left to walk beside the forest, and pause to read a notice about Beacon Hill Common, and also notice where the earthwork known as the **Short Ditch** crosses.

Turn left down to Llugwy Farm if a campsite is required.

Beacon Hill Common is part of the Crown Estate and extends for 1889 hectares (4667 acres). It is designated Access Land, and Glyndŵr's Way crosses it for some 8km (5 miles). The boggy area where the River Lugg rises is a Site of Special Scientific Interest. Radnorshire Wildlife Trust holds

A clear track rises gently onto the Crown Estate moorlands of Beacon Hill Common

a conservation lease on the moorlands, which are notable for bird-watching. The boggy areas suit snipe and curlew, while the heaths are populated by grouse, skylark, ring ouzel, whinchat, wheatear and meadow pipit. Buzzards, peregrines and hen harriers might be spotted hunting. Moorland vegetation includes heather, bilberry and crowberry, with bracken abundant in some places and a few rare plant species present in specific areas. The moors provide grazing for sheep, while grassier areas are favoured by cattle and ponies.

Theories abound as to the origin of **Short Ditch**. It really is short, measuring no more than 300m in length, across a broad gap. Some claim it was constructed around the same time as Offa's Dyke, in the late eighth century. Others say that the ditch was cut by Edmund Mortimer, in the hope of preventing Owain Glyndŵr from reaching Knighton. Whether or not that is true, Glyndŵr destroyed the castle in Knighton in 1402.

Follow the track gently uphill beside a fence, with a field to the left and moorland to the right. Pass a corner on the fence and stay on the most obvious track over a moorland crest, around 480m (1575ft), beside **Pool Hill**. Walk gently down across a broad, gentle dip, watching for marker posts at intersections with lesser paths, to be led across a broad moorland gap of grass and

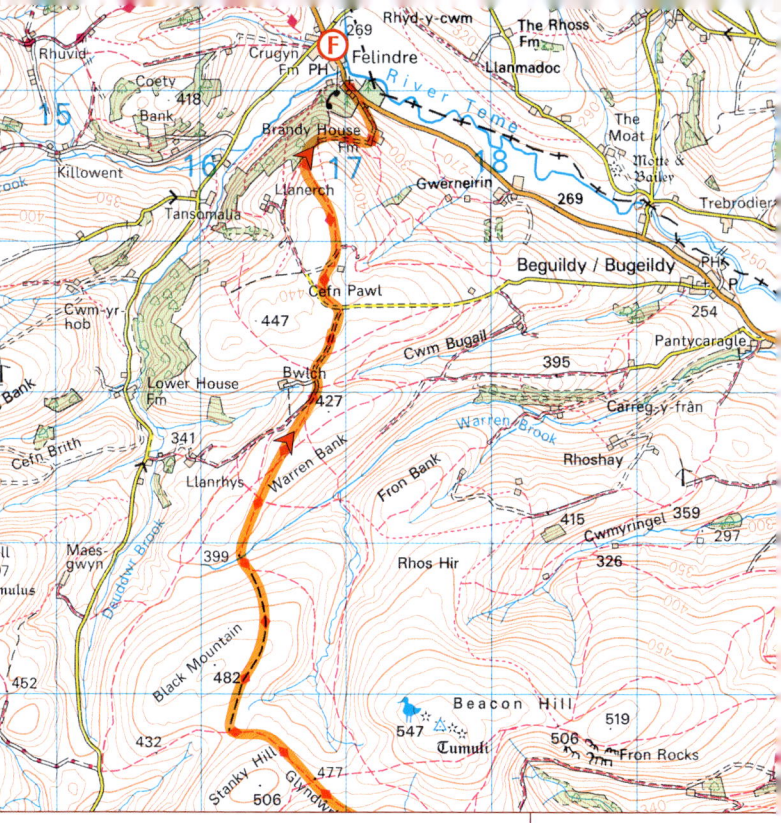

heather beside **Beacon Hill**. The path runs into a dip to cross a small stream, then rises. Eventually, two grassy tracks join and continue as a clear, firm track around the shoulder of **Stanky Hill**, again around 480m (1575ft). There is a descent to a broad and boggy gap, where a marker post indicates a right turn.

Watch for marker posts as the path climbs onto the shoulder of **Black Mountain** to around 470m (1540ft). Drop down to another gap, passing beside what looks like a wood, but is actually the overgrown remains of hedgerows that once surrounded a few small fields. Cross a footbridge and climb gently, still watching for marker posts on **Warren Bank**. Pass a signpost on this grassy moorland crest

Descending from Brandy House Farm to the little village of Felindre

and rise gently a little further before descending gently to a muddy track on a broad gap. Go through a gate within sight of the isolated farmhouse of **Bwlch**, and follow the track uphill with wide-ranging views.

Reach a junction with a narrow minor road at **Cefn Pawl**. Cross over and head diagonally left as marked. A grassy path follows a fence around a few fields to reach a signpost. Take careful note of the direction indicated for Felindre, as markers are a bit sparse for a while and the path is vague. However, walk across the slope and head downhill to find a gate on the right. Go through and cross a field, picking up a track winding down to **Brandy House Farm**. The farm access road descends quickly to the little village of **Felindre**, where a left turn along the road leads to the Wharf Inn.

FELINDRE

Felindre is small and compact, sitting beside the River Teme in a pleasant agricultural valley.

Lodgings are limited to Brandy House Farm and Trevland, which both offer camping, indoor accommodation and breakfast. The Wharf Inn serves drinks only, further into the village. The nearest little post office shop is at Beguildy, nearly 3km (2 miles) off-route along the B4355 road.

DAY 2
Felindre to Abbeycwmhir

Start	Wharf Inn, Felindre
Finish	Happy Union Inn, Abbeycwmhir
Distance	25km (15½ miles)
Ascent	690m (2265ft)
Descent	700m (2295ft)
Time	8hr
Terrain	Valleys, farmland, hill pastures, more rugged hills and woodland
Maps	OS Landranger 136
Refreshment	Wharf Inn at Felindre. Community Shop at Llanbadarn Fynydd. Happy Union Inn at Abbeycwmhir
Transport	Daily Traws Cymru buses link Llanbadarn Fynydd with Newtown, Llandrindod Wells, Builth Wells and Merthyr Tydfil.

Farm tracks and field paths cross grassy hills, over and over again, between the villages of Felindre and Llanbadarn Fynydd. There is an opportunity to break for food and drink at the New Inn at Llanbadarn Fynydd, or puzzle over why a long-vanished roadside weighing machine should be commemorated by gilt-inlaid stone tablets! The route crosses the shapely hills of Moel Dod, Yr Allt and Ysgŵd-ffordd, before dropping into a wooded valley. The delightful little village of Abbeycwmhir is named after a large abbey, of which very little remains.

Leave **Felindre**, around 270m (885ft), by walking up to a nearby crossroads and turning left. Almost immediately, turn right through a farmyard and turn right again to pass behind Upper House. ▶ Follow the winding track up through gates and fields. When the track runs out, continue up and along a grassy crest, later crossing the top of a hill at almost 400m (1310ft). A line of hawthorn trees, an old hedge, leads down the grassy crest to a gate, where a clear enclosed track leads further downhill to a farm called **Rhuvid**.

This is not a right of way, but the landowner allows access on foot.

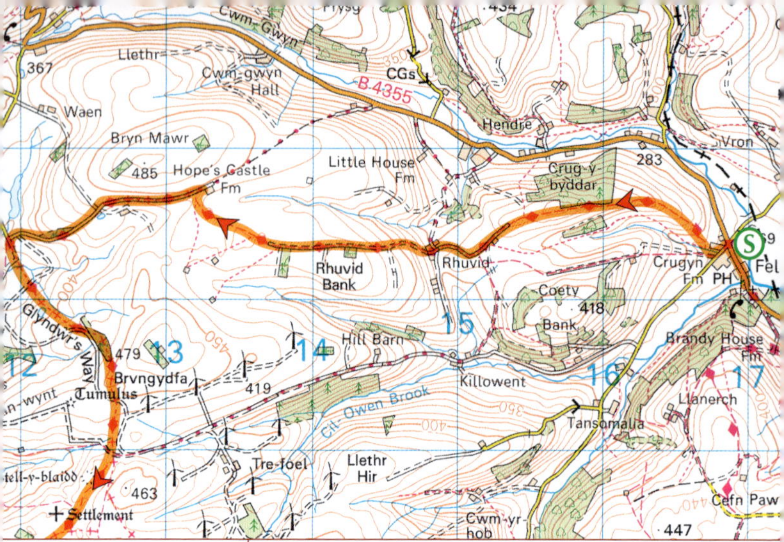

Go straight through the farmyard, through a gate and straight up a broad stony track, sometimes worn to bedrock. Pass a small plantation high on **Rhuvid Bank**, around 440m (1445ft). Continue ahead along the broad crest, and the firm surface gives way to a grassy surface, passing some attractive Scots pines. Go through a gate and continue ahead, quickly turning right on a track. Reach a junction with a minor road near **Hope's Castle**

Scots pines stand beside a grassy track on the way towards Hope's Castle Farm

DAY 2 – FELINDRE TO ABBEYCWMHIR

Farm and turn left. Follow the road, flanked by trees at first, passing above a solitary farmhouse, then wind downhill to reach a prominent bend in the road.

Turn left along and down a track. When the track suddenly bends right, keep straight ahead past a gate and stile to cross a footbridge over a small stream. Climb along a vague, wheel-rutted grassy track, through gates and through a small Scots pine plantation. Go through a gate at the top of the plantation and drift right of a fence crossing a grassy crest, over 450m (1475ft), on **Bryngydfa**. Cross a footbridge over a muddy ditch, look ahead and go through a gate, then follow marker posts across a field, later crossing a track.

Wheel-ruts cut by tractors show the way through a gentle gap between grassy hills. Join a track, then the route later goes through a gate beside trees. Look back at the profile of **Castell-y-blaidd**, whose earth rampart is best seen from this point. ▶ Continue following the wheel-ruts ahead and head gently up to a gate, signposts and a minor road. Turn right to follow the road along the crest of **Fron Top**, reaching an altitude of 456m (1495ft). There are distant views of the Bannau Brycheiniog and Eryri national parks.

The road runs downhill and eventually passes a farm. Stay on the road all the way downhill, later passing the

Castell-y-blaidd translates as 'wolf's castle', and is thought to be a Norman defensive enclosure, possibly unfinished; it contains no trace of any internal structures.

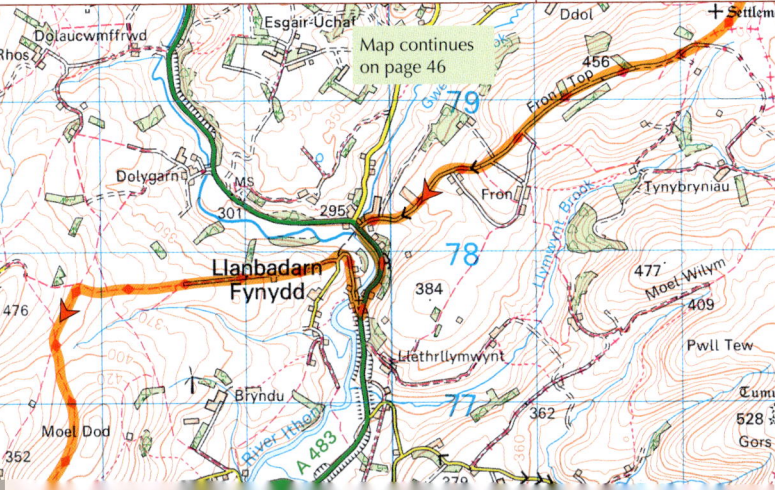

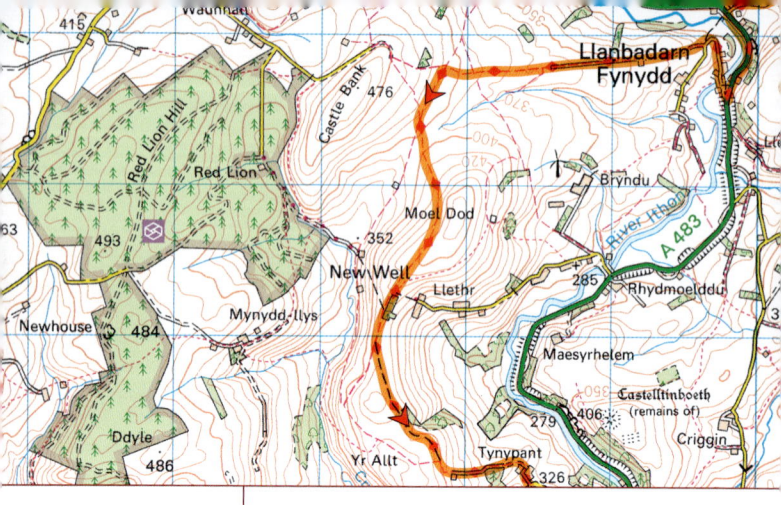

access track for a house and continue down to a junction with the main A483 road at **Llanbadarn Fynydd**, around 300m (985ft). Turn left to follow the main road, or if wet feet can be endured, shortcut across a ford on the **River Ithon**.

LLANBADARN FYNYDD

At first glance there seems little of interest here, but the area abounds in ancient earthworks, as well as being on the course of a Roman road. An odd stone monument commemorates a long-forgotten weighing machine. When the road was improved by William Pugh of Bryn-Llywarch in 1823, he installed a weighing machine. In 1885, William B Pugh of Dolfor removed the machine and a monument was put up to commemorate it. When the road was widened, the monument had to be moved, so an additional inscription records that this was done by Edward Minton-Beddoes of Dolfor, in 1930 – another momentous occasion for Llanbadarn Fynydd!

Although the church of St Padarn, from which the village takes its name, is a 19th-century 'restoration', a church has existed here since the 12th century. Curiously, although the village name translates as 'St

Day 2 – Felindre to Abbeycwmhir

Padarn in the mountain', an earlier rendering translated as 'St Padarn in the desert'.

There is a Community Shop, just out of sight in the direction of Newtown. Daily Traws Cymru buses link the village with Newtown, Llandrindod Wells, Builth Wells, Merthyr Tydfil and Cardiff.

The signposted route passes above the church of St Padarn, using the main road, before turning sharply right along a minor road and passing below it. However, it is possible to cut the corner and walk down through the churchyard. Either way, follow the minor road across the river, then climb from the village, turning left around a bend.

Turn right as signposted up a clear track, flanked by hedges, eventually reaching a gate beside a stand of larches. Go through the gate and climb gently beside a fence on a grassy slope. Climb most of the way towards

St Padarn's Church at Llanbadarn Fynydd

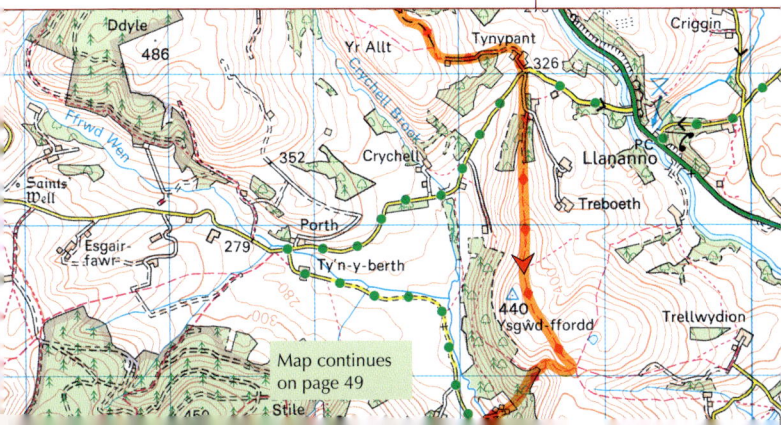

Map continues on page 49

a clear-felled plantation on **Castle Bank**, but turn left as marked at a gate and stile, and walk alongside another fence. Go through another gate and walk straight ahead. Marker posts indicate a grassy path through bracken, which leads to a footbridge on a broad and boggy gap.

A grassy path climbs past gorse bushes, and there are several wet, muddy, boggy patches to negotiate. Keep an eye on marker posts, which climb over the shoulder of **Moel Dod**, around 450m (1475ft), where there is a view of the distant Brecon Beacons. Head down towards a small forest, crossing a track on a gap. Continue as marked alongside a grassy embankment and fence, with a line of contorted larches going the same way. The fence gives way to a drystone wall, and the wall quickly gives way to a forest fence, but the path pulls away from it, flanked by masses of gorse bushes. Pass through a hollow on the hillside and continue along another fence accompanied by larch trees, across the slopes of **Yr Allt**.

Go down through a gate near a white house and walk down a track through more gates, passing through the farmyard at **Tynypant**. Turn left down to a crossroads on a gap at 326m (1070ft). Walk straight through and climb to a stand of conifers, where Bwlch Farm comes into view. Turn right as signposted through a gate, heading up a grassy track alongside the forest, then level out briefly to go through a gate near where the forest ends. A fine grassy track climbs onwards, usually flanked by grass

A fine grassy path, flanked by heather, reaches almost to the summit of Ysgŵd-ffordd

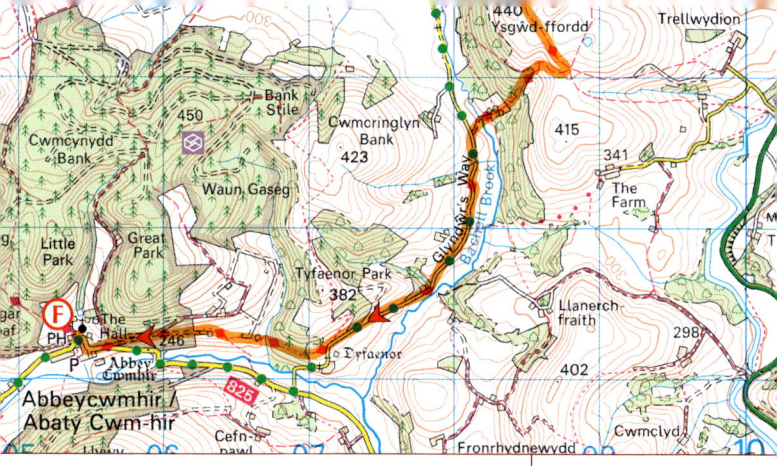

and gorse, and eventually passes well to the left of the trig point on **Ysgŵd-ffordd**. ▶

Head gently downhill, keeping right at a waymarked fork, then turn right as marked at a path intersection on a gap. Wind downhill to another junction and turn left, going more steeply downhill. Go through a small gate to continue down through mixed forest. Emerge at some buildings and walk down an access road. Either follow the road across a concrete bridge over **Bachell Brook**, around 250m (820ft), or walk a few paces upstream to cross a footbridge bearing Glyndŵr's Way markers. Either way, walk up to a road junction and turn left to follow an undulating minor road through a pleasant pastoral valley, enjoying views.

The road eventually drops close to the river, where there is a bridge to the left and a corrugated iron hut to the right. Follow the road steeply up a wooded slope, then later there are valley views again. Just as the road starts to drop steeply towards an old farm at **Dyfaenor**, turn right as signposted up a few wooden steps and cross a stile into a field. Aim straight across the sloping field for the biggest tree seen ahead. Once closer to it, head for a stile to the right and cross into a wood. Follow a path to a pile of slate from a landslip. Don't cross it, but drop down to the left, cross a stile and turn right, then drop again and cross two footbridges over a stream and its tributary.

Climbing to the 440m (1445ft) summit takes only a couple of minutes, and the views are extensive.

Climb and go through a gate, then keep to the top side of a field. Go through a gate as marked and climb above a house, passing it before going down through a gate onto its access track. Turn right and follow the track away from the house into forest. Join a tarmac road and turn left to follow it down to a junction with a minor road. **The Hall** stands nearby, but follow the road past Home Farm and into the little village of **Abbeycwmhir**, around 260m (855ft).

ABBEYCWMHIR

The Cistercians originally founded their abbey nearby in 1143, but abandoned it and started again on the present site in 1176. No doubt they felled trees during its construction, but much of the area has been reforested with commercial plantations. The Mortimer family had an interest in the site, as did King John. From 1227, Llywelyn Fawr supported the building of a much grander structure. The ground plan of the nave suggests that this would have been one of the largest in Britain, but it was never finished. The monks supported Llywelyn ap Gruffydd, who was slain in battle against Edward I in 1282. Although Llywelyn's body is said to be buried somewhere on the site, having been secretly removed from grisly display in London, this

Very little remains of the abbey at Abbeycwmhir, which has been plundered for stone for several centuries

Day 2 – Felindre to Abbeycwmhir

has never been proven. Despite the abbey becoming a pilgrimage centre, this didn't prevent it being sacked by Owain Glyndŵr in 1401, who suspected the monks favoured Henry IV. Ultimate ruin came after the Dissolution, under Henry VIII.

Stonework from the abbey can be found in nearby structures, including The Hall, St Mary's Church and the farm of Dyfaenor, which was originally a hunting lodge. Five whole arches were taken to Llanidloes to extend St Idloes Church in the mid-16th century. There is an interesting one-room exhibition about the abbey at Home Farm, although very little is left of the actual ruins. For more information see abbeycwmhir.org.

The Hall, built in Victorian Gothic Revival style in 1834 by Thomas Wilson, was doubled in size by the Philips family in 1869, and its 52 rooms have been restored and sumptuously furnished since 1997, when the Humpherstons acquired it. There are 5 hectares (12 acres) of Victorian gardens. While members of the public were able to visit The Hall in the past, tours are no longer available.

Facilities in and around Abbeycwmhir are limited to the Happy Union Inn, which incorporates a part-time post office. No meals, but soup and sandwiches can be ordered in advance. B&B options include Laurel Bank and The Oaks. A campsite is also available at Home Farm.

An old petrol pump opposite the Happy Union Inn

GLYNDŴR'S WAY

DAY 3
Abbeycwmhir to Llanidloes

Start	Happy Union Inn, Abbeycwmhir
Finish	Market Hall, Llanidloes
Distance	25km (15½ miles)
Ascent	760m (2495ft)
Descent	850m (2790ft)
Time	8hr
Terrain	Forests, farmland, hill pastures and a succession of wooded valleys
Maps	OS Landranger 136
Refreshment	Happy Union Inn at Abbeycwmhir. Café at Bwlch-y-sarnau. Plenty of choice at Llanidloes.

After leaving the forested environs of Abbeycwmhir, Glyndŵr's Way crosses the grassy Upper Esgair Hill and passes through the tiny settlement of Bwlch-y-sarnau. More forestry plantations occupy the central part of this stage, then tracks and paths slice across open slopes, offering splendid views deep into the heart of Wales, with views stretching from the Bannau Brycheiniog to the Eryri national parks. The route later zigzags in and out of wooded valleys, then a final road-walk leads straight into Llanidloes – the first town since leaving Knighton.

Leave **Abbeycwmhir** from the Happy Union Inn. There is an old petrol pump across the road, as well as a signpost pointing up an access track. Follow the track, quickly reaching a house, and go through a gate to continue straight ahead along a sunken grassy track. Go through another gate into a forest and climb to a track junction on a gap between the little hills of **Sugar Loaf** and **Y Glôg**. Walk straight ahead and downhill, and keep straight ahead at any junctions in the forest. Cross a footbridge over a river and climb to a road.

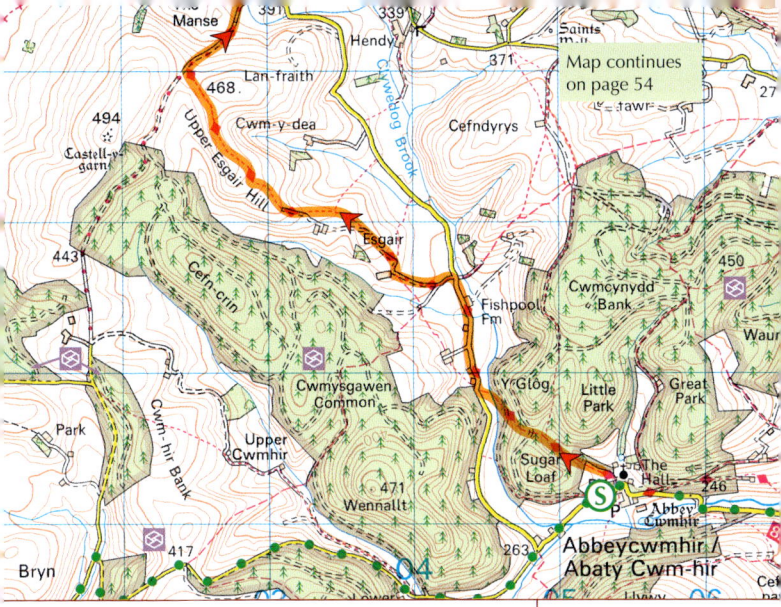

Glyndŵr's Way used to go through a nearby farm, but the right of way through the farmyard has been disputed, so turn right and follow the road past **Fishpool Farm**. ▶ Turn left as marked at a road junction and follow the road uphill, bending right and left past **Lower Esgair**. The tarmac ends later, and a gravel track runs level, with a view of another farm ahead. However, go through a small gate on the right as marked, and follow a hedge and fence alongside a field. Follow a hedge through the next field too, completely avoiding the farm, then go through a gate onto a track.

Turn right to follow the track uphill and go through a gate at the top into a field. Climb diagonally right to reach a gate in a fence, but don't go through. Instead, turn left to follow the fence and go through a small gate in a corner. Immediately turn right to follow another fence, still climbing on **Upper Esgair Hill**. Cross another field and watch for another small gate marked on the right, giving access to a small field, around 450m (1475ft). Leave the field and continue parallel to the fence on the left, then later make a beeline just to the left of a small coniferous

The fishpool was established by monks from Abbeycwmhir.

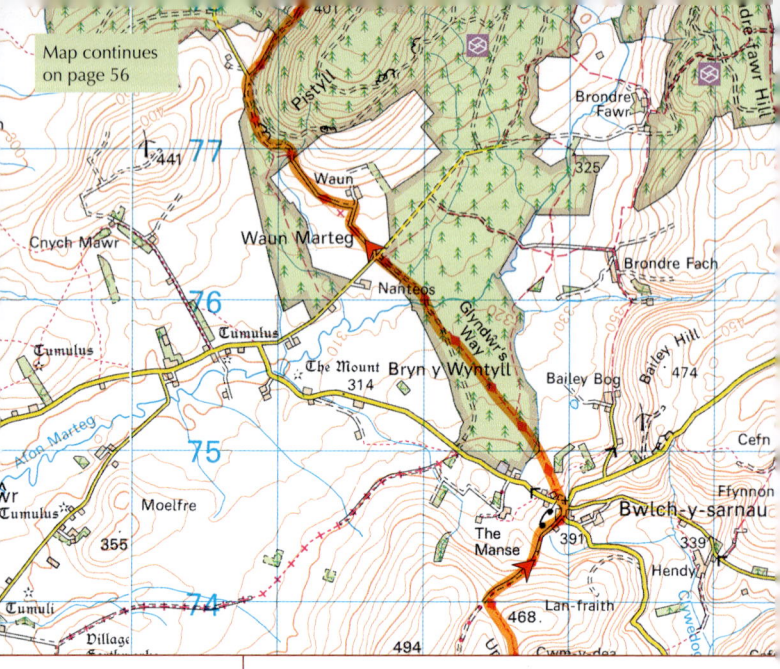

plantation near a gap. Join a clear stony track and turn right to follow it downhill. It crosses a gap, then climbs to a road junction at **Bwlch-y-sarnau**.

Keep left along the road, passing a few houses to reach the Baptist Church and Community Centre. The centre incorporates the Glyndŵr's Way Café. ◄ Just beside a telephone kiosk is a gate. Go through it and down a track, then go through another gate to the right of a house. Continue down through a field, through yet another gate, and later cross a footbridge on the left. Follow a path into forest at **Bryn y Wyntyll**, which is level or gently sloping downhill, wet and boggy in places. Eventually, a firm track is joined. Turn right to follow it and cross a concrete bridge over the **Afon Marteg**, around 310m (1015ft). The track rises gently to a gate and a minor road. Turn left and immediately reach a road junction, then turn right as signposted for Llydiart-y-waun.

The road rises and winds past fields, passing below a farm called **Waun**, then runs through forest. When another

The porch is open from Easter to early November for DIY snacks and drinks, with an honesty box for payment. The full café can be pre-booked by groups.

Day 3 – Abbeycwmhir to Llanidloes

farm can be seen ahead, outside the forest, fork right as signposted along a track and remain inside the forest. The track rises to a turning space above the farm of **Prysgduon**, above 400m (1310ft), then descends to a junction with its access track. Turn right and rise along the track, descend to cross a stream, rise again, then descend to a track junction and cattle grid above **Trinnant**. Climb again, keeping right of Esgair-Fedw, and walk up a tarmac road. The road levels out and crosses a cattle grid, then begins to fall.

Turn right along a signposted track, beside farm buildings. Head down into a valley, cross a footbridge over a stream, and climb above ruins and below a quarried face at **Grach**. Follow the track as marked, which is rough and stony. When gates are reached, go through the one up to the right. Climb across a field and go through another gate. Rise across a field, following a tumbled drystone wall and marker posts on the slopes of **Pegwn Bach**, around 420m (1380ft). There are fine views across rolling hills, fields and woodlands, with the more distant uplands of Pumlumon and the Eryri national park featuring.

Turn left down a grassy track, through a gate, and down a track and road. Climb a little to a signposted road junction, where there is an old washing mangle, and turn right. Follow the road up between farm buildings to go through another gate, turning left. When the tarmac appears to end, turn left and quickly right along tracks

A track descends from the slopes of Pegwn Bach after a fine traverse across hillsides

Glyndŵr's Way

made of broken tarmac. Cross a cattle grid and continue down the track to a gate and ruined building. Follow the winding track to ford a little stream, then rise through a gate and continue to another gate and a signposted track junction above **Cnydfa**, around 390m (1280ft).

Turn left down through yet another gate, following the track as it winds steeply down into an attractive valley, almost reaching a river near **Cwm**, around 230m (755ft). Turn left upstream, as signposted, along a wooded track that can be muddy. Cross a footbridge and climb, but don't go through a gate. Instead, follow a vague, grassy path further upstream, but well above the river, to reach a marker post and a stile. Cross the stile and keep left of two holly

trees in a field, climbing a steep grassy slope to another marker post and stile. There are fine views back across the valley, now revealing the extent of the Llandinam Wind Farm.

> Operated by Scottish Power Renewables, **Llandinam Wind Farm** could be changing shape in future. Opened in 1992, over 100 turbines were planted on a moorland site encompassing 1307 hectares (3230 acres), in excess of 500m (1640ft) above sea level. There is a plan to remove these turbines and replace them with 34 new ones, although these would be more than twice the height of the existing machines. The 'repowering' of the site would also require the construction of pylon lines and substations to deliver the extra energy to the National Grid.

Turn left up a track and climb to a minor road, then turn right up the road and follow the tarmac until it levels out and expires. Cross a cattle grid and fork left uphill at a track junction. Cross a crest around 380m (1245ft), then descend. Keep straight ahead, avoiding two left turns, following a fence down a grassy slope. Watch out for a tall marker post and turn left, keeping left to follow a grassy track beside another fence. Watch for more markers and muddy patches, and pass a solitary house.

Cross a stream in a dip beyond the house, then climb, watching for a marker post and a gate into a field. Cross a little stream and reach a signpost on a bend on a track. Turn left to walk up the track, and watch for a path leaving it on the right later, crossing two stiles. Walk across a rushy area, crossing a grassy track. Head down to a small gate and go through it into a field, turning right to walk gently uphill. Go through two more small gates, then turn left and go through another small gate. Veer right to climb slightly across a field, joining a track near a house on the shoulder of **Moelfre**.

Turn left to walk down the track a short way to a junction, and go through a gate into a field. Walk down

Newchapel Baptist Church – built, rebuilt, restored, destroyed by fire and rebuilt again

Camping available.

through this field, and another field, then turn right as marked alongside yet another field. Drop steeply into a wooded ravine and cross a footbridge. Climb from the wood, then go through gates through two fields to reach a road-end at a house called Ashfield. Turn right up the road, reaching a junction with another road at Prospect Farm. Turn right downhill, reaching another road junction. Turn left here and pass the Baptist Church at **Newchapel**. Note the chapel date-stone, which records: 'Founded in 1740. Rebuilt 1815. Restored 1905. Destroyed by fire 1954. Rebuilt 1957.'

Walk down past mobile homes at Woodland View and down to a house at Cwm. ◄ Just past the house, turn left into a yard, go through a gate, then turn left down beside a field to a stile. Cross over it and wind down a woodland path to cross a footbridge over a stream. Wind uphill and round into another wooded valley to cross a small stream, then walk up through a gate to leave the wood. Bear left up through a field and cross a stile beside a signpost to reach a road bend. Turn right to follow the minor road along the foot of **Gorn Hill**.

A bunkhouse is passed at Plas Newydd, then the road begins to descend noticeably. Go down through

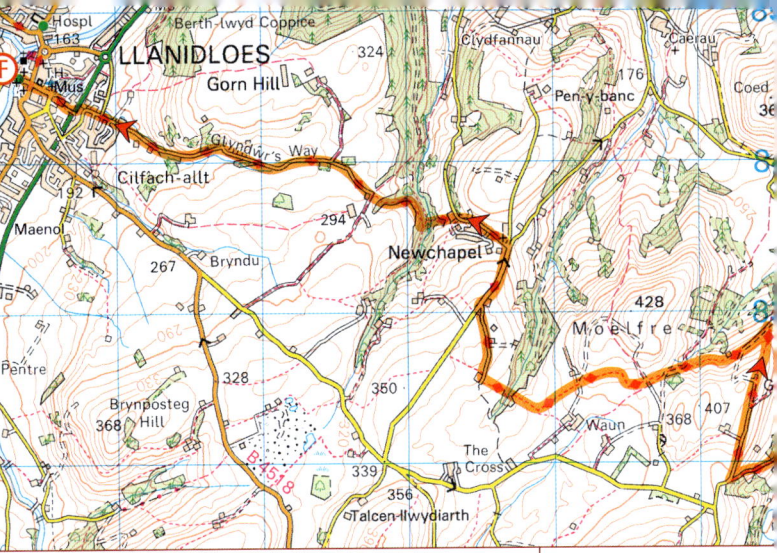

a wooded valley and cross a stream, then houses come into view. Follow the road down into the suburbs, and once the road is forced left, turn right as signposted along a path. Cross a footbridge over the A470 road that bypasses **Llanidloes**. ▶ Head straight along Maesyllan to reach a road junction, and turn left, then right, to continue straight along Great Oak Street to the

The road follows the course of an old railway line that closed in 1962.

LLANIDLOES

Llanidloes sits in the centre of the ancient kingdom of Arwystli and is named after the seventh-century St Idloes. In Norman times, a motte and bailey was constructed on a site now occupied by the Mount Inn. A market charter was granted in 1280 by Edward I, and the old market cross was replaced with the Market Hall in the 1600s. This striking black-and-white brick and timber building sits squarely in the heart of the town, slowing the traffic and occasionally being hit by it! There is a stone at one corner of the building where John Wesley is said to have preached in 1748, 1749 and 1764.

Most of the buildings in the centre are Georgian and Victorian, dating from times when the town enjoyed prosperous periods. Llanidloes was a thriving centre for the textile industry, peaking during the late 18th century, but the town suffered wavering fortunes in the early 19th century. Around this time, the Chartist movement was growing and was very strong in the area. When three Chartists

GLYNDŴR'S WAY

were arrested in 1839 and held at The Trewythen Arms Hotel in Great Oak Street, a mob assembled and a riot ensued. Troops had to be called in and the town was virtually garrisoned for a year. Following the development of nearby lead mines at Van and Bryntail in the mid-19th century, the population of Llanidloes virtually doubled.

Having walked from Abbeycwmhir to Llanidloes, it is worth visiting St Idloes Church to see the five stone arches that were transported over that distance from the old abbey to be incorporated into the building in the mid-16th century. The Llanidloes Museum is in the Town Hall on Great Oak Street. It focuses on the past three centuries of local history, and also has a section on nature and forests. The Renaissance-style Town Hall, built in 1908, has served a multitude of purposes. It once was a temperance hotel, and now houses a market hall.

Llanidloes has a full range of services, including accommodation, nearby campsite, shops, pubs, restaurants, post office, cashpoints and taxis. Bus services operate daily, except Sundays, reaching places such as Newtown, Welshpool, Shrewsbury, Rhayader, Llandrindod Wells and Aberystwyth. National Express coaches link Llanidloes with Aberystwyth, Welshpool, Shrewsbury, Birmingham and London. After Llanidloes there are no more bus services available until Machynlleth is reached, two days further along Glyndŵr's Way.

black-and-white Market Hall in the town centre, around 170m (560ft).

Be sure to have a plan in place before leaving Llanidloes. The next town is Machynlleth, which takes two days to reach on foot. The natural halfway point is around the tiny villages of Staylittle and Dylife, where accommodation is quite sparse. If lodgings cannot be secured, it might be necessary to arrange a pick-up with an accommodation provider some miles off-route. If a taxi is likely to be required, be sure to check that one will be available before starting walking.

DAY 4
Llanidloes to Dylife

Start	Market Hall, Llanidloes
Finish	Dylife
Distance	22km (13¾ miles)
Ascent	890m (2920ft)
Descent	650m (2130ft)
Time	6hr 30min
Terrain	Woodland, farmland, an extensive reservoir, forest and grassy moorland
Maps	OS Landranger 136
Refreshment	Plenty of choice at Llanidloes. Shop off-route at Staylittle.
Transport	None at any point between Llanidloes and Dylife.

The gentle hills outside Llanidloes were plundered for lead ore and other minerals, primarily in the 18th and 19th centuries. The ruins of the Bryntail Lead Mine lie at the foot of the Llyn Clywedog dam. The reservoir was constructed in the mid-1960s and fills a convoluted valley, so it keeps appearing in view as other hills and valleys are crossed. Somewhere around Staylittle or Dylife, in another former lead-mining area, walkers will finish their day before reaching the highest stretch of Glyndŵr's Way.

The River Severn, or Afon Hafren, known to the Romans as Sabrina, is the longest river in Britain. It rises on the boggy moorland slopes of Pumlumon and reaches the sea via the enormous Severn Estuary between Bristol and Cardiff. The **Severn Way** attempts to follow the river as closely as possible from source to sea, from Pumlumon to Bristol, along a route measuring 360km (224 miles). Llanidloes is the first town on the river, and for a short stretch across the slopes of Allt Goch Glyndŵr's Way and the Severn Way run concurrently.

Start at the Market Hall in the centre of **Llanidloes** and follow Long Bridge Street to a roundabout. Turn left to cross the bridge spanning the River Severn, then turn left again as signposted for Staylittle and Machynlleth, along Westgate Street. Walk up the road, passing two turnings on the right for Tan-yr-Allt, then turn right along a signposted path. Pass an information board that explains about the woodlands of **Allt Goch**. Alien coniferous species have been reduced in favour of native broadleaved species such as oak, beech, birch, hazel and holly, although sycamore is also present.

Keep straight ahead at all junctions, continuing straight up a track, and reach a broad turning area among tall beeches. Descend slightly, but turn left as marked to follow a path up through woods, crossing a track. The path gradually swings left and runs beside a golf course, reaching a tarmac road at the **club house**. Pass the club car park and turn left into a wood. Turn right to walk alongside two fields then turn right along a track. Turn left to walk away from farm buildings at **Penhallt**.

Watch for a marker post pointing left over a stile near a gate and walk down alongside a field. Continue down

The River Severn as seen on the way out of Llanidloes

past a couple more stiles and gates, then turn right, heading down through a field to reach a gate onto a minor road. Turn right down the road, then cross a stile on the left as signposted near a house. Drop downhill, looking for stiles from one field to another, and eventually reach a gate onto another minor road. Walk straight ahead along the access road towards **Garth**.

Before reaching the buildings, watch for a marker post on the right, which reveals a path up a wooded slope. Join and follow a track ahead, alongside a field, passing tall conifers. Climb towards the top of the field and cross a stile beside a gate, next to a small quarry. Keep to the right-hand side of the grassy hill, and look northwards to spot two chimneys at the old **Van Mines**. Go through a gate to leave the field and follow an old track flanked by trees. Go through a gate and turn left as marked, then turn right as marked to walk gently uphill alongside fields. The idea is to keep away from nearby buildings and walk parallel to an access track to reach the **B4518** road.

Turn right and walk along a gravel path beside the road, down to a road junction on a gap. Walk straight

ahead at the junction and climb a little, then turn left off the road and right through a gate. Follow a path uphill, parallel to the road but high above it, across the slopes of **Penwar**, around 310m (1015ft). Descend gently to a gate in a fence to reach a signpost and road junction.

Turn left to follow the access road towards **Bryntail**. Before reaching the farm, a signpost points right towards a gate. Go through this and aim to keep away from the farmhouse before crossing a track and dropping to another track near outbuildings. Follow the track towards a forest, then descend in sweeping bends with views of the concrete dam of **Llyn Clywedog**. Go through a gate as marked to reach the ruins of **old lead mines** below the dam, and spend time exploring these.

> The **former lead mines** are made up of a series of four lead-mining areas – Aberdaunant, Bryntail, Pen y Clun and Van. They basically exploit the same geological formation across a span of 4km (2½ miles). Apart from the two chimneys spotted earlier

near Van, the Bryntail ruins below the reservoir dam are the most significant and the safest to explore.

The Bryntail and Pen y Clun mines were the first to start production in the early 18th century, but this quickly stalled. After another start in the mid-19th century, it was the subsequent development of the Van mines that delivered the greatest wealth, employing up to 700 men and requiring the installation of lots of machinery and waterwheels. However, despite initially producing much lead and zinc, as well as a little silver, the reserves were quickly exhausted, and the mines were closed early in the 20th century. In the declining years, the mining enterprise passed through many hands and lost a great deal of money. In its heyday the industry resulted in the doubling of the population of Llanidloes and the construction of a railway line, although the branch serving the mines closed in 1940.

Cross a footbridge over **the Afon Clywedog**, around 210m (690ft), turning right and bending left up to a car park. Walk up a road and reach a junction. Turn right and follow the road steeply uphill to another junction. Turn

The peaceful little village of Van, where a very busy and noisy mine once operated to the left

Caffi Clywedog is usually open at weekends, Friday to Sunday, for lunch.

right again to reach a fine viewpoint overlooking the dam of Llyn Clywedog. ◄

A bronze relief map of **Llyn Clywedog** reservoir and the hill country it occupies should be studied. Various statistics are recorded, which can be compared with Llyn Efyrnwy on Day 7.
- Height of dam: 72m (235ft)
- Length of dam: 229m (752ft)
- Maximum depth of water: 65m (212ft)
- Level of spillway: 283m (927ft) above sea level
- Volume of water impounded: 50,000 million litres (11,000 million gallons)
- Surface area: 250 hectares (615 acres)
- Length of reservoir: 10km (6 miles)
- Catchment area: 46km^2 (18 square miles)
- Construction commenced: 6 April 1964
- Impounding commenced: 22 Dec 1966

Walk along the road (or the viewing wall) until a road bend is reached. Go through a small gate and climb a path beside a tumbled wall. ◄ Join the road to cross a cattle grid, around 370m (1215ft), then walk down the road to a house called Ty Capel, which offers B&B, and turn right. A path runs down beside a field, with a fine view of the middle reaches of the reservoir, but views are lost as the path goes through a small gate. Two footbridges are crossed close together later, and a path is followed around an arm of the reservoir, crossing another footbridge. Follow the shore path round a point to reach a bend on a track, then keep left to follow the track above the **Clywedog Sailing Club**.

The hill just to the south, Pen-y-Gaer, is crowned by an Iron Age hill fort.

Walk up the access road a short way, then turn right to pick up and follow another shore path. After crossing a footbridge, climb up a partly wooded slope and aim for the highest corner of a long, steeply sloping field. Go through a gate and enjoy a fine view of the reservoir, then as the path descends, it reaches a tall marker post where an exceptionally long stretch of the reservoir can be studied. When the path reaches a road,

Day 4 – Llanidloes to Dylife

Clywedog Reservoir is quite convoluted, so it appears in view for a few hours of walking

cross over and go through a gate as signposted. Follow a grassy track across a field and ford a stream. A stony track rises through a couple of fields, then the idea is to contour across fields, where the path is vague, looking for marker posts and gates, before dropping to cross a footbridge over a stream.

Turn left and go through a small gate into clear-felled forest. The path soon turns right and climbs to another small gate. Go through it and turn left, rising alongside a field. Either watch for a marker post or, as soon as a house comes into view, climb to the right and go through yet another small gate on the forested slopes of **Banc y Groes**. Turn left up a track and later keep right at a junction with a track serving the house. Later, watch for a marker post on the right of the track and climb a little to leave the forest via a gate, around 390m (1280ft).

Walk down a moorland slope, which can be wet in places, but aim for a gate to the left of a small plantation, where a firm track leads down through another gate. Soon afterwards, leave the track and keep left of a couple of gates, dropping towards a stream and passing left of a building to reach a gate onto a minor road. Turn left to follow the road across a bridge spanning the **Afon Biga**. Shortly afterwards, turn right as signposted along a forest track.

The forest path continues, climbing **Fign Aberbiga** with one last view of Llyn Clywedog, even though the reservoir extends further to Staylittle. Reach a road and turn right to follow it through the forest, heading down past wooden chalets and the Hafren Forest Bunkhouse at **Dolydd** to leave the forest and cross a bridge over the **Afon Llwyd**.

> Note the **'limestone doser'** to the left, which aims to counteract the acidity of the river by periodically releasing crushed limestone into the water.

Follow the bendy road uphill until a signpost points left. Go through a gate and follow a very degraded tarmac track alongside a field. Go through another gate and

Day 4 – Llanidloes to Dylife

follow a marker pointing away from the track to cross a footbridge. Walk up to a gate and up a stony track, turning right as marked along a grassy track above the farm of **Nant-yr-hafod**. Go through a gate, and later drop as marked to go through another gate into a lower field. Turn left and walk through fields, from one marked gate to another, later crossing a farm access track at **Llwynygog**.

> Use this track to reach the nearby village of Staylittle, if the post office shop or accommodation at The Lodge is required. A local blacksmith was said to work so quickly that anyone needing their horse shod would only have to 'stay a little'.

Keep just to the right of the farm buildings, where gates lead onto a fenced, hedged track. Follow this and go through a gate into a field and bear slightly left to follow a fence. Go straight ahead through gates as marked

to reach a farm access track where it crosses a bridge over the **Afon Clywedog**. Walk up the road a little, but avoid the farm by keeping left as marked, climbing through small gates, then following a broad grassy track uphill. This quickly narrows to a deeply sunken path, but follow it faithfully until directed left through a small gate into a field.

Turn right to climb through another small gate into another field. Keep climbing until the tops of forest trees are seen bristling ahead, then a kissing gate will be seen in a fence. Cross a track just before going through the kissing gate, then turn left up another track. This rises gently, with views of the Eryri national park – along with almost every major wind farm development in mid-Wales. The track is often worn to bedrock, which features vertically bedded slates. Go through a gate, where the accompanying fence switches from the right-hand to the left-hand side of the track. Cross a crest around 440m (1445ft) to reach a slight dip. Unless you have accommodation booked far, far ahead, this is the last opportunity to leave the trail. Turn right at a junction and follow a track down to a minor road at **Dylife**. Y Star Inn provides

A track descends from Glyndŵr's Way to the roadside at Dylife

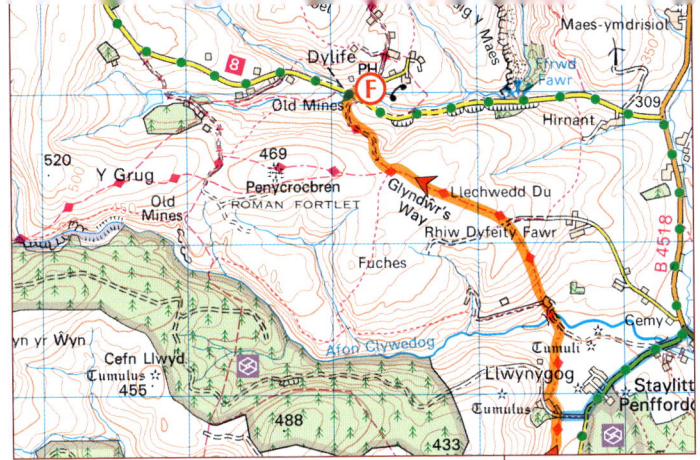

self-catering accommodation here, even for walkers on Glyndŵr's Way who might only be staying for one night, but bear in mind that if you stay for two nights you could also use this as a base for climbing Pumlumon Fawr.

DYLIFE

The earliest attempts to exploit lead reserves around Dylife may date back to Roman times, but more concerted efforts began in the 17th century, with peak production occurring in the mid-19th century. At that time, Dylife was a thriving township with up to 1000 inhabitants, with pubs, post office, shop, chapels, church and a school. The largest waterwheel ever seen in Wales, the 'Martha', was installed to pump water from the mines. Once the industry went into decline in the late 19th century, buildings were demolished one by one, leaving only the scattered hamlet that today's visitors see.

Y Star Inn was formerly a droving inn. It offers self-catering accommodation on this remote stretch of Glyndŵr's Way and might soon operate as a pub again. The only other lodging nearby is a shepherd's hut, which has to be booked through Airbnb, requiring a two-night stay. A further option involves arranging a pick-up and drop-off with the Old School House B&B, off-route at Pennant.

Ascent of Pen Pumlumon Fawr

Start/Finish	Dylife
Distance	26km (16 miles)
Ascent/Descent	550m (1805ft)
Time	9hr
Terrain	Mostly open and exposed moorlands, boggy in places, sometimes pathless, but with navigation aided by following fences
Maps	OS Landranger 135
Refreshment	None
Transport	None

This optional ascent of the highest 'mountain' in mid-Wales involves a day-long there-and-back route from Dylife. Alternatively, walkers can stay on Glyndŵr's Way and continue straight to Machynlleth (Day 5). Pumlumon Fawr is actually a vast sprawling moorland, its highest point being Pen Pumlumon Fawr, anglicised as Plynlimon. Reaching it from Glyndŵr's Way involves a long, hard day's walk across bleak and boggy moorlands. In mist it would seem like a treadmill, but navigation is made easy because most of the route follows fences along the moorland crest. There are very few rights of way, but the bulk of the route is across designated Access Land. Pumlumon means 'five summits', and it is also the source of three rivers – the Severn, Wye and Rheidol – that chart remarkably different courses to the sea.

Start on the roadside at **Dylife**, at a gate beside a small red postbox. A signpost bearing a Cambrian Way marker points straight up a clear track. The track climbs and soon reaches the crest of a hill, where there is a signpost for Glyndŵr's Way. Turn right and follow another track up through a gate, rising gently and passing through another gate. There is an aerial on the right, and on the left lies

ASCENT OF PEN PUMLUMON FAWR

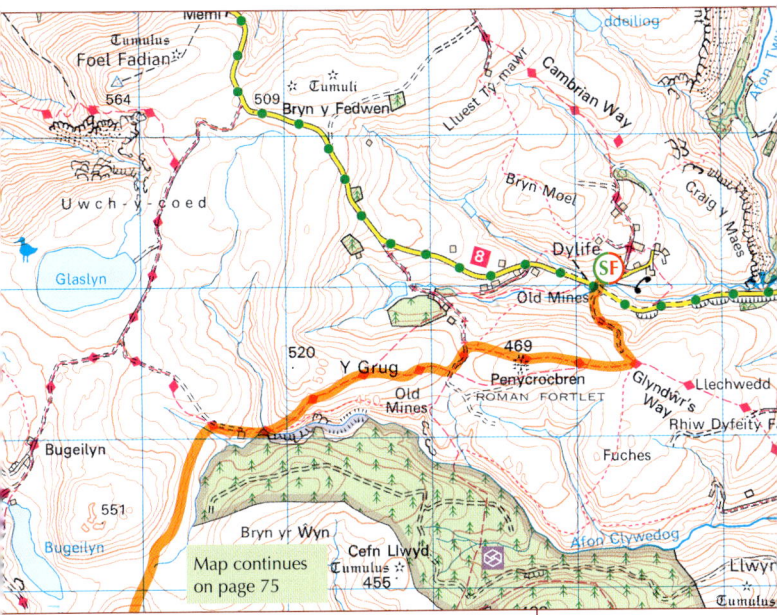

the low square embankment of a Roman fortlet, at 469m (1539ft), on **Penycrocbren**.

Penycrocbren translates as 'gallows hill' and is in one of those remote places usually associated with public execution. Local lore relates that around 1700 a blacksmith known as Siôn y Gof left his wife and family to work at Dylife. Later they came to visit him, but by that time he was involved in an affair with a local woman. Siôn killed his wife and children and threw them down a mineshaft, but their bodies were later discovered, and Siôn was sentenced to be hung and gibbeted. As he was the only blacksmith in the area, he was forced to make his own gibbet. In 1938 the remains of a gibbet and skull were discovered, and these are now in the Welsh Folk Museum in Cardiff

Looking ahead, the broad moorland slopes of Pumlumon fill the horizon. Follow the track onwards downhill, through a gate, to reach a junction with another track. Glyndŵr's Way heads left, quickly joining another track, following it gently uphill through yet another gate. Walk downhill, then turn right through a small gate into a big field on the slopes of **Y Grug**. Follow a grassy embankment up through the field and go through another small gate. Continue across a grassy moorland slope, which is designated Access Land, where the path levels out then descends through yet another small gate. Drop into a valley and cross a footbridge over a stream, near a small waterfall.

Climb to a building and follow a track up across the moor, noting a memorial stone to the right. Step to the left and follow a sheep path, picking up an old watercourse that leads towards a mine ruin. Cross a stream before reaching the ruin and continue along the sheep path, rising gently across a boggy moorland slope to join a clearer sheep path. Follow this onwards, and it begins to swing to the right at almost 500m (1640ft). Leave the path and head directly southwards across an untrodden boggy area, aiming for a junction of three fences.

Follow the fence that heads southwards, climbing up a heathery slope, passing a junction of three more fences. Keep right and keep climbing, gently at first, then a little more steeply. Reach yet another junction of three fences at 622m (2040ft) on **Carnfachbugeilyn**. There is a shelter-cairn here, as well as a boundary stone dated 1865. ◄ Views encompass two little reservoirs at Bugeilyn, extensive moorlands in all directions, and the more mountainous skyline of the Eryri national park.

More of these boundary stones will be seen throughout the ascent.

Turn right to follow the fence onwards, and it later turns left round a corner in sight of a conspicuous cairn made of white quartz boulders. Later, a path crosses the fence via a stile, offering a detour to the right to the cairn. However, it is worth turning left to cross the stile and pick up a flagstone path that leads to a prominent wooden post. This marks the **source of the River Severn** in a boggy pool around 610m (2000ft). ◄ Whether or not the short

The river can be followed from source to sea using Terry Marsh's guide The Severn Way, *also published by Cicerone.*

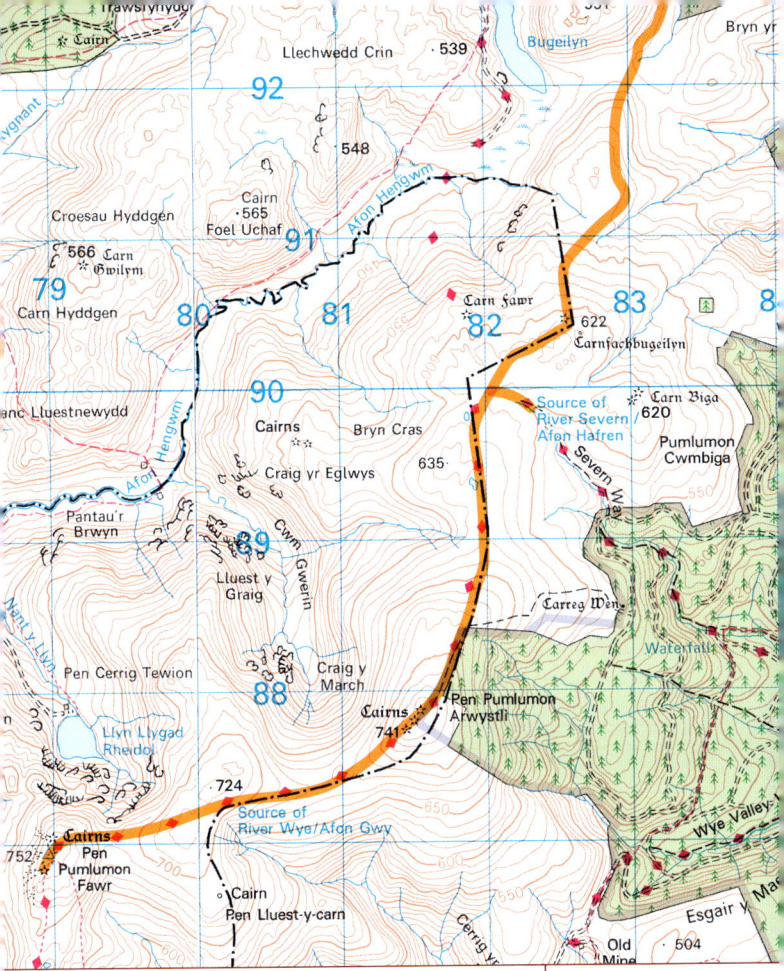

detour is taken, continue following the fence, passing another junction of fences, and keep rising gently.

Little pools are passed among boggy hollows and extensive swathes of heather. Pass one of the '1865' boundary stones near a pool, where the fence turns a slight corner. Keep rising, later on firmer ground, passing a gate and yet another junction of fences, where there

GLYNDŴR'S WAY

One of the distinctive boundary stones along the way

The Roman fortlet on Penycrocbren, with Pumlumon to the left

is a stile. Later, a small cairn and a boundary stone are reached near the corner of a fence at 690m (2265ft). Leave the fence and follow wheel marks through the grass, gradually drifting back towards the line of the fence as height is gained. Leave the fence again to follow marker posts towards two sprawling summit cairns on **Pen Pumlumon Arwystli** at 741m (2430ft).

Pick up and follow a path downhill, gradually converging with the line of the fence on a broad gap around 680m (2230ft). Climb beside the fence and go through a gate at a junction of fences. Keep straight ahead along the trodden path, passing a small summit cairn and boundary stone, beside a fence corner, over 720m (2360ft). The **source of the River Wye** and the Rheidol are nearby. Follow the fence down across a gap, where there is a cairn around 690m (2265ft). Climb beside the fence and head straight for the big boulder summit cairn, cairn-shelter and trig point on **Pen Pumlumon Fawr** at 752m (2470ft). Enjoy the extensive views, then retrace footsteps faithfully back to **Dylife**.

ASCENT OF PEN PUMLUMON FAWR

Although Pumlumon is far from Glyndŵr's Way, Hyddgen lies just to the north, where the important **Battle of Mynydd Hyddgen** was fought by Owain Glyndŵr. Although precise details of the battle and its location are scanty, it took place in 1401, when Glyndŵr's forces, measuring anything from 120 to 500 men, were camped in a valley. A superior armed force, comprising English and Flemish settlers from Pembrokeshire, outnumbered them by three to one. The Welshmen were lightly equipped and able to move swiftly across rugged, boggy terrain, while their enemies moved slowly and were at a distinct disadvantage. This resulted in a notable early victory for Glyndŵr.

THREE RIVERS

According to an old story, Father Pumlumon had three daughters – Hafren, Wye and Rheidol. When they were due to leave home, he promised them as much land as they could cover between dawn and dusk on a single day. On the appointed day, Hafren hurried away at the break of day and managed to cover an enormous distance before reaching the sea. Wye woke later, and with less time available, took a more direct route to the sea, but still had the time to cover some distance. Rheidol woke very late, and realised she would have to dash straight for the sea or risk getting no land at all!

As a result, Hafren (Severn) is the longest river in Britain, charting a circuitous course, well endowed with sweeping meanders, and claiming a huge amount of land. Wye claims less land, but nevertheless includes charming countryside and occasional meanders. Rheidol is short and direct, spilling directly westwards in a headlong rush to the sea.

GLYNDŴR'S WAY

DAY 5
Dylife to Machynlleth

Start	Dylife
Finish	Parliament House, Machynlleth
Distance	25.5km (16 miles)
Ascent	830m (2725ft)
Descent	1240m (4070ft)
Time	8hr
Terrain	Open moorland, valleys, farmland, hills and forest
Maps	OS Landranger 135
Refreshment	Y Star Inn off-route at Dylife. Plenty of choice at Machynlleth.
Transport	None at any point between Dylife and Machynlleth. Aberhosan, off-route, has an occasional bus link with Machynlleth. Machynlleth has rail services, linking with the coast at Aberystwyth and Pwllheli, and heading inland to Newtown, Welshpool, Shrewsbury and Birmingham. Bus services from Machynlleth reach Bangor, Dolgellau, Aberystwyth and Newtown.

Glyndŵr's Way climbs over a broad moorland gap, passing close to the isolated moorland lake of Glaslyn and the rugged hump of Foel Fadian. The moors extend southwards to Pumlumon, which may already have been explored (see above). Valleys come one after the other during this stage, with a couple of steep climbs between them. There are no services apart from a solitary B&B until the town of Machynlleth is reached. This remote settlement was the seat of Owain Glyndŵr's short-lived Parliament, where he was crowned Prince of Wales in 1404.

Start on the roadside at **Dylife**, at a gate beside a small red postbox. A signpost bearing a Cambrian Way marker points straight up a clear track. The track climbs and soon reaches the crest of a hill, where there is a signpost for Glyndŵr's Way. Turn right and follow another track up through a gate, rising gently and passing through another

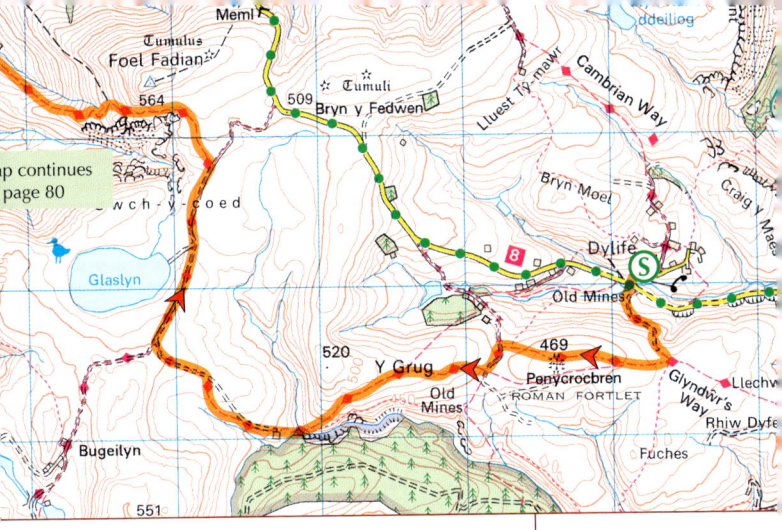

gate. There is an aerial on the right, and on the left lies the low square embankment of a Roman fortlet, at 469m (1539ft), on **Penycrocbren**.

Looking ahead, the broad moorland slopes of Pumlumon fill the horizon. Follow the track onwards downhill, through a gate, to reach a junction with another track. Glyndŵr's Way heads left, quickly joining another track, following it gently uphill through yet another gate. Walk downhill, then turn right through a small gate into a big field on the slopes of **Y Grug**.

Follow a grassy embankment up through the field and go through another small gate. Continue across a grassy moorland slope, which is designated Access Land, where the path levels out then descends through yet another small gate. Drop into a valley and cross a footbridge over a stream, near a small waterfall.

Climb past bare rock to reach a track and pass well to the right of a large building. Follow the track up across the moor, noting a memorial stone to the right. Fork left as marked along a grassy track, passing mine ruins where the little stream was once dammed to provide power. This enterprise was a costly failure in the mid-19th century. Re-join the main track and turn left, following the track up to a junction at 500m (1640ft). Turn right to walk

gently downhill, then over a gentle rise, with a view of the lake of Glaslyn to the left. After a gentle descent, keep straight ahead at a cattle grid and track junction.

The lonely moorland pool of **Glaslyn** is managed as a nature reserve by the Montgomery Wildlife Trust. It is easily reached by following a short path, and walkers can make a complete circuit of the shore. The surrounding moorlands are home to red grouse, skylark, wheatear and ring ouzel. Wildfowl are attracted to the pool in winter. The acidic water is a poor habitat, but the unusual quillwort grows in it, at its southernmost limit in Britain.

Rise gently along the track and turn left as marked at a junction. Keep climbing and reach the highest point on the whole of Glyndŵr's Way, almost touching 510m (1670ft) on the southern slopes of **Foel Fadian**. Note the yellow marker posts indicating a path to the summit at

564m (1850ft), which is a fine viewpoint – both northwest to Cadair Idris and southwards to Pumlumon. The path overlooks a deep, steep-sided, stony ravine at the head of the Afon Dulas. Descend steeply along the path, which now features bare rock that may be wet and slippery, or covered in loose stones. Turn left at a junction and continue winding down to a gate, where the Access Land ceases.

A fine grassy track runs downhill through another gate and along the wooded edge of a valley. Go through a gate at a track junction, now walking on broken slate, and continue down through woods. There is a road bend at the farm of **Nantyfyda**, then continue down across a bridge and up to a road junction. Turn right, steeply uphill, then continue at a gentle gradient past fields. A signpost points left for Machynlleth. ▶

Turn left along a grassy track, which may be muddy in places, and continue through fields. Watch for a marked right turn, where the path has gorse bushes to the right,

The high, remote lake of Glaslyn is easily reached by detouring a short way off Glyndŵr's Way

The nearby tiny village of Aberhosan has an occasional midweek bus link with Machynlleth, but this must be booked in advance.

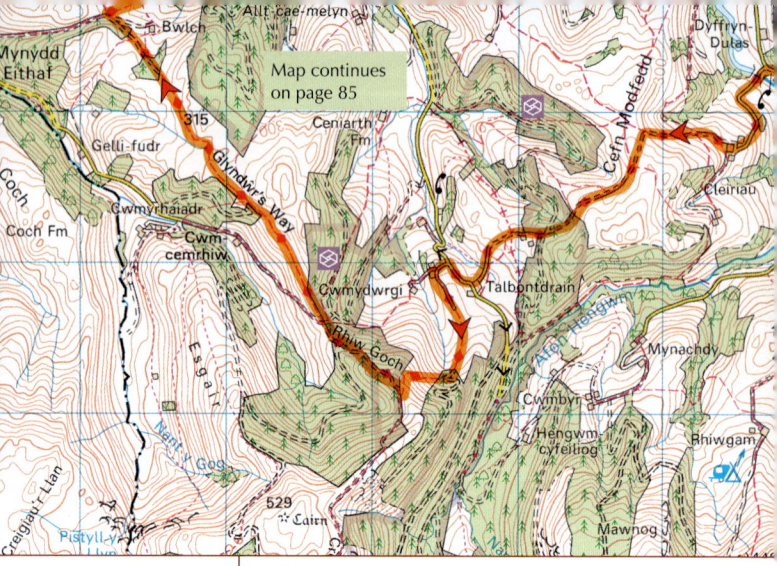

Map continues on page 85

heading down through woods to a minor road. Turn right to follow the road across a slope planted with oaks. Pass a junction where there is a telephone kiosk, then turn left at the next junction, before **Dyffryn-Dulas**. Cross a bridge, around 90m (295ft), then follow the road steeply uphill. It bends left and right, with good views back across the valley and up to Foel Fadian and neighbouring heights.

Go through the farmyard at **Cleiriau Isaf**, then at a gate immediately afterwards turn sharp right and climb steeply a short way to another gate. Enter a field and keep to the right-hand side, passing above the farm and going through yet another gate. Turn left to follow a track uphill, through more gates, bending left as marked. Go through a gate beside a plantation on the slopes of **Cefn Modfedd**, over 270m (885ft), then follow the track gently downhill and go through another gate.

Fork left as marked, going up and along a grassy track beside a fence, then downhill. Go through a gate into a forest and continue downhill. Cross a forest track, and the track being followed reaches a gate soon afterwards. Go through it and follow a grassy track, forking right downhill at a junction, among gorse bushes. Walk down through a gate, where there is a building to the left, and continue down among trees and fields through another gate. Cross a ford and walk up to the farmhouse of **Talbontdrain**, offering B&B, keeping left of it to reach a minor road. Turn right along the road, going up a little, then downhill.

A track leads down from Foel Fadian to Esgair-Fochnant

Looking across the valley above Cwmydwrgi, where Rhiw Goch lies to the right

A path climbs off-route, up through a groove that later features slippery slate, known to horse-riders and mountain-bikers as The Chute.

Turn left along a track, then fork left at a track junction just before a white house. The track rises past fields and goes through gates, including a gate into a forest. However, turn right, in effect straight ahead, to follow a grassy path to the edge of the forest, and cross a stile beside a gate. The path climbs across a grassy slope, following an earth embankment and ditch, with fine views of the valleys and the mountains beyond. Reach a marker post and fence beside a clear-felled forest and turn left uphill, passing through a gate at **Rhiw Goch**, around 360m (1180ft). ◀

Turn right, as marked, to follow a stony path that drops from clear-felled forest to still-standing forest, passing through a gate onto a grassy gap. Cross a track at a gate and signpost, and continue straight ahead uphill. Don't walk too close to the forest fence, but keep a few paces away from it, passing a marker post before drifting left up to another wooden post. Follow a stony path that cuts across a grassy hillside, generally rising gently and sometimes flanked by gorse bushes. Pass the corner of a fence, go through a gateway, and later ford a little stream in a wet and boggy area.

The track later runs down through a gate into forest, quickly leaving through another gate, then going through yet another gate into another forest. Walk down to a track junction and turn right, not along a track, but through a gate, to walk downhill beside a fence into a valley

A short detour offers a view of little Llyn Glanmerin

Day 5 – Dylife to Machynlleth

below **Bwlch** at 200m (655ft). Climb a little, then turn left as indicated by a marker post, to climb a steep grassy slope, watching for more markers. These lead to a small gate into a clear-felled forest, where a clear track leads onwards, undulating gently above 260m (855ft). Keep left at a junction later, descending to pass through a gap in a drystone wall into still-standing forest. Descend further and leave the forest through a small gate at **Parc**. ▶

Follow a path that rises alongside the forest, then heads slightly right at a marker post, winding away from the forest on slopes of grass, bracken and gorse. Eventually, there are views down to Machynlleth, shortly

A short detour left, back into the forest, reveals a path offering a view of nearby Llyn Glanmerin.

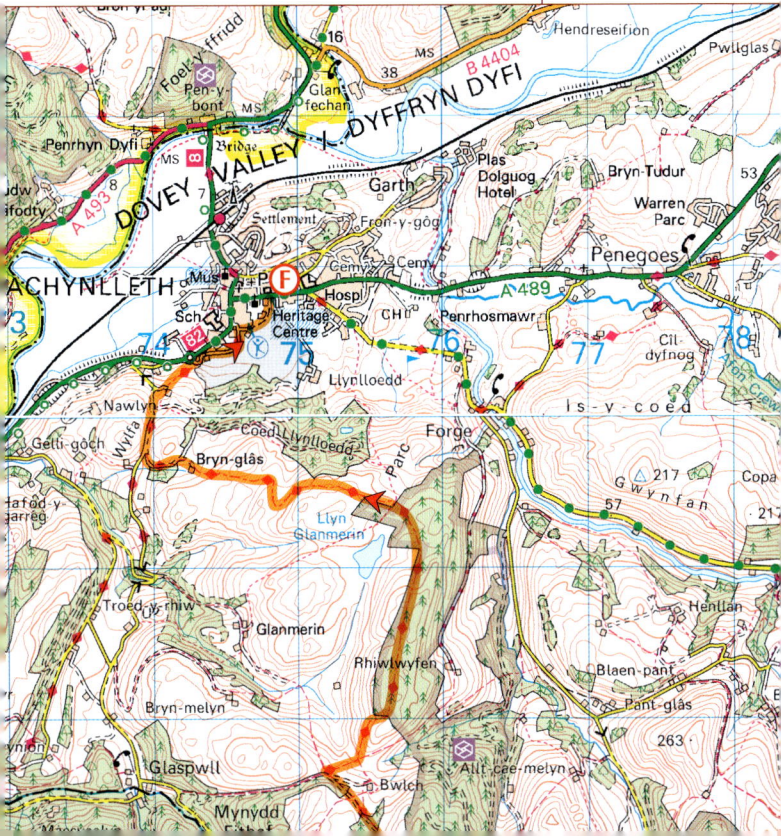

GLYNDŵR'S WAY

before the path passes through a large gate. Follow a clear track that winds as it descends, passing through a little gap between hills. Go through another large gate and descend through woods, emerging at a house called **Bryn-glâs**.

A track junction is reached beyond the house. Turn left, down through a gate into woods, and later join a minor road. Follow this straight ahead over a rise, then downhill until a signpost points right. ◀ Follow a path downhill, passing near a white house and crossing its access track. The path runs down through a kissing gate, then down the 'Roman Steps', carved into the slate bedrock. Reach a road at the bottom, very close to sea level, and turn right through a gateway along a park access road. Walk straight ahead as marked, and later the tarmac path bends left to pass a large building called **Y Plas**. ◀ Turn right and walk straight ahead past a leisure centre, and the tarmac path bends left to reach a busy road in the centre of **Machynlleth**, facing the Parliament House.

> The Wales Coast Path briefly follows the same course as Glyndŵr's Way here.

> Note the large stone commemorating Owain Glyndŵr, inlaid with a gold disc.

> Anyone with an interest in 'green' issues might like to break their journey at Machynlleth and visit the nearby **Centre for Alternative Technology**, which is 4km (2½ miles) out of town on the road towards Corris. The centre has been developed since 1973 in an old quarry. Interesting eco-cabins can be hired where visitors can keep an eye on their personal energy consumption during their stay. There are plenty of hands-on displays and equipment, much of it made from recycled materials, exploring practical solutions for the generation and conservation of energy. A low-energy house can be investigated, and Britain's largest 'green' bookshop is on site. See www.cat.org.uk.

MACHYNLLETH

With five days to practise pronunciation, first-time visitors to Machynlleth should be able to get it more or less right on arrival. Alternatively, the name is

DAY 5 – DYLIFE TO MACHYNLLETH

Owain Glyndŵr's Parliament House in the heart of Machynlleth

often abbreviated to 'Mach'. The area has a long history of settlement, embracing Bronze Age and Roman times. A market charter was granted in 1291 by Edward I. However, the town is chiefly remembered for being the seat of Owain Glyndŵr following his coronation as Prince of Wales in 1404. The Parliament House (www.canolfanowainglyndwr.org) is associated with the establishment of Glyndŵr's parliament and with his coronation. The Royal House, now a fine café, was where Dafydd Gam was held prisoner after plotting an assassination attempt on Glyndŵr.

There are plenty more interesting buildings around town, most notably the mansion of Y Plas, which is passed on the way into town. This was the home of the Marquess of Londonderry from the mid-19th century. The building was gifted to the town in 1948, along with parkland containing many tall trees, where a variety of sports facilities and a leisure centre are available. The imposing clock tower in the town centre, formally named the Castlereagh Memorial Clock, was erected in 1874 to celebrate the 21st birthday of Viscount Castlereagh, eldest son of the Marquess of Londonderry.

Machynlleth has a full range of services and is a centre for art and culture. There is a range of accommodation, as well as shops, pubs, restaurants, post office, cashpoints and taxis. There is a railway station, linking with the coast at Aberystwyth and Pwllheli, and heading inland to Newtown, Welshpool, Shrewsbury and Birmingham. Bus services reach places such as Bangor, Dolgellau, Aberystwyth, Tywyn and Newtown. Buses also serve points further along Glyndŵr's Way, such as Penegoes, Cemmaes Road and Llanbrynmair.

DAY 6
Machynlleth to Llanbrynmair

Start	Parliament House, Machynlleth
Finish	Wynnstay Arms, Llanbrynmair
Distance	26km (16 miles)
Ascent	850m (2790ft)
Descent	700m (2295ft)
Time	8hr
Terrain	Roads and low farmland, hill pasture, valleys, forest and grassy moorland
Maps	OS Landranger 125, 135, 136
Refreshment	Plenty of choice in Machynlleth. Dovey Valley Hotel at Cemmaes Road. Wynnstay Arms Hotel and Caffi JoJo at Llanbrynmair.
Transport	Regular buses link Machynlleth, Penegoes, Cemmaes Road and Llanbrynmair with Newtown, daily, except Sundays.

The course of Glyndŵr's Way plays hide and seek with the Dyfi valley for half a day. However, the first stretch from Machynlleth to Penegoes is low level, so views are confined. Later, views northwards from Bryn Wg and Cefn Côch reveal the length of the valley, with mountainous Eryri beyond. After leaving Cemmaes Road, the route climbs between little hills and valleys, then passes through a forest to emerge on a moorland shoulder. From there it is all downhill, and the little village of Llanbrynmair lies just off-route.

Leave the centre of **Machynlleth** by following Heol Maengwyn, the A489 Newtown Road, eastwards. Turn right along a minor road signposted for Llyn Clywedog, Llanidloes, Forge, Aberhosan and Dylife. The road quickly leaves town and rises to a cattle grid and gate. ◄ The road crosses an open common used as a golf course, crosses another cattle grid and

Note a protected trig point on the left, securely fenced.

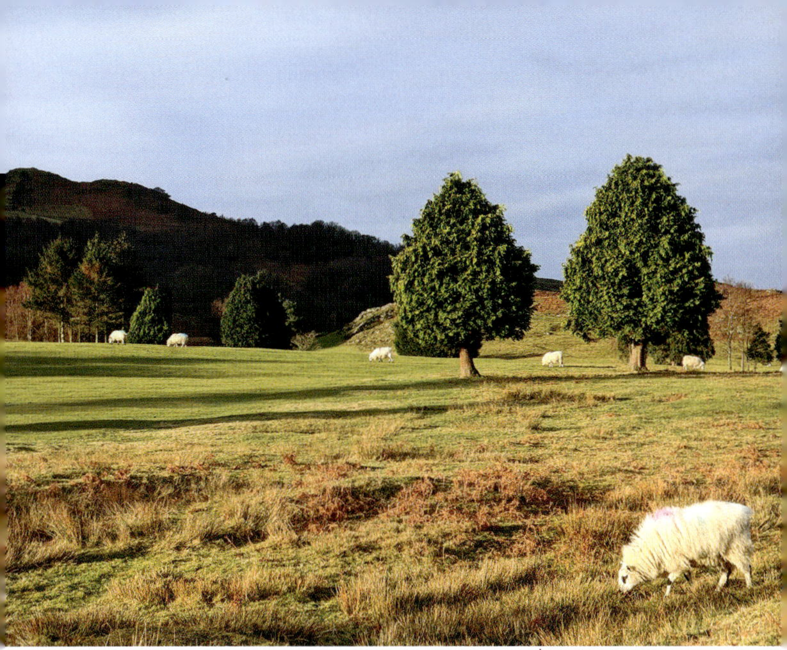

continues to the little village of **Forge**, where there were once many fulling mills. Turn left as signposted for Aberhosan and Dylife, crossing a bridge over the Afon Dulas. Keep following the road, passing the Cwm

View from the road crossing the golf course on the way out of Machynlleth

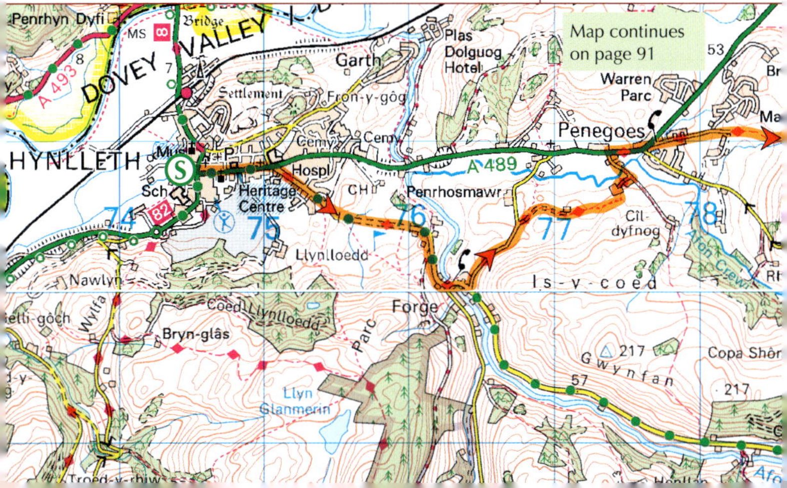

Map continues on page 91

Dylluan B&B. Turn left as signposted up another road, leaving the village.

A signpost points right, where a track crosses a cattle grid into a field. Don't follow the track all the way to a farm, but turn right uphill as marked. Go through a small gate beside a water trough, then look ahead to spot another small gate beside a large gate. Follow marker posts on a slope to reach a track. Turn left down through gates, then turn right at farm buildings and follow the track to join a minor road. Turn left down the road and cross the **Afon Crewi** to pass a fine 17th-century mill building, Felin Crewi. The road leads to the main **A489** road, where a right turn leads into the little village of **Penegoes**. ◀

> Bus services link the village with Machynlleth, Cemmaes Road and Llanbrynmair, except Sundays.

The main road bends left, then Glyndŵr's Way turns right along a minor road signposted for Maesperthi Caravan Park. The road climbs to **Maesperthi**, but just before reaching it, a track climbs on the right. This is patchy concrete and grass at first, linking with a gravel track later. Follow this across a dip, then fork left at a junction to climb. The track passes through gates, levelling out at a gate. Turn left as indicated up a steep grassy slope, following a fence over the top of **Bryn Wg** at almost 200m (655ft). Drop to two gates close together and go through them, then follow a path along a brow, overlooking slopes of bracken, then golden gorse bushes, then bracken again. Enjoy views across the Dyfi valley to southern Eryri.

> The **Dyfi Biosphere Reserve** covers a huge area, embracing the entire catchment of the Afon Dyfi from sea to source. Walkers following Glyndŵr's Way enter it above Dylife and leave it halfway between Llanbrynmair and Llangadfan. The aim of the reserve is to explore ways in which the local heritage, culture and the economy can thrive in harmony with the natural environment. The lower part of the Dyfi valley was designated as a Biosphere Reserve in the 1970s, but the wider

catchment area was included in 2009. See **biosfferdyfi.org.uk**.

Walk down through a small gate and cross a dip in the slope, then rise to continue along the brow. Marker posts show the way across a track and through a small gate, then a grassy ribbon of a path descends a slope of bracken. The path twists and turns below the hillside cottage of **Bryn-wg-isaf**, generally falling, but occasionally rising. There are fine views of a little village, but these are lost as the path winds down through woods. Go through a small gate and along an enclosed path. Join a minor road and turn left to follow it. Watch for a path signposted on the left, revealing a footbridge over the Nant Gwydol, beside the old woollen mill of Yr Hen Felin. Quickly climb into **Abercegir**, where the village is full of cosy terraced houses.

Turn left up the road, then right at a junction to follow another road. A signpost points left up a track for Fronfraith. This climbs as a gravel track, but changes to concrete. Watch for a small gate marked on the left. Go through it and climb to the top of a field, then look ahead for more gates and markers. After a steep climb through

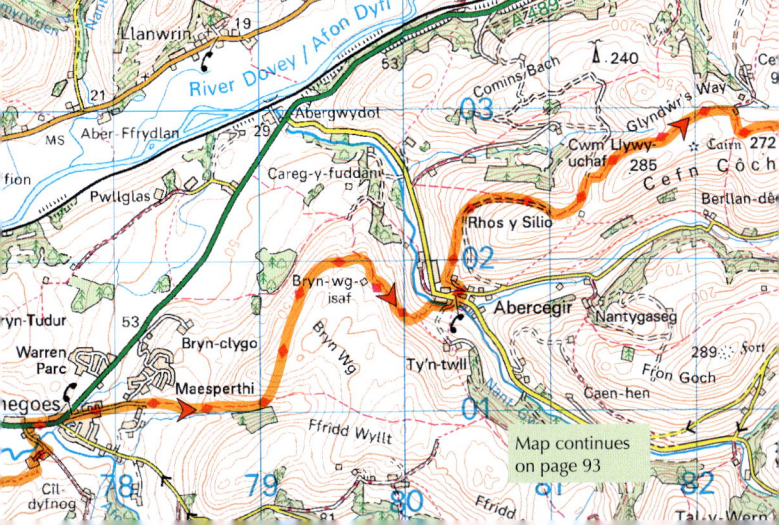

Map continues on page 93

a field, go through a small gate in a drystone wall and climb to join a broad, clear grassy track. Follow this up through a gate until it expires at another gate on **Rhos y Silio**. Walk downhill, watching for Glyndŵr's Way markers to continue. Later, a marker capped with a yellow plastic cap points right up another track, which quickly bends left and climbs more gently, around 260m (855ft), on **Cefn Côch**.

When the track expires at a gate, go through and veer slightly left, gently downhill. Pass a marker post and head uphill and downhill, passing more marker posts, to link with a track above the farm of **Cefncoch-gwyllt**. Turn right uphill, through a couple of gates, bearing left and more or less levelling out through more gates, while passing from field to field. A gate leads onto a track. Walk down to a gate and a junction with a minor road.

Turn left down the road, then soon turn right to leave it as signposted. Walk gently up through a field from one small gate to another on **Cefn Côch**, touching 200m (655ft), then steeply downhill while watching carefully to

The little village of Abercegir, nestling in a valley at the foot of Rhos y Silio

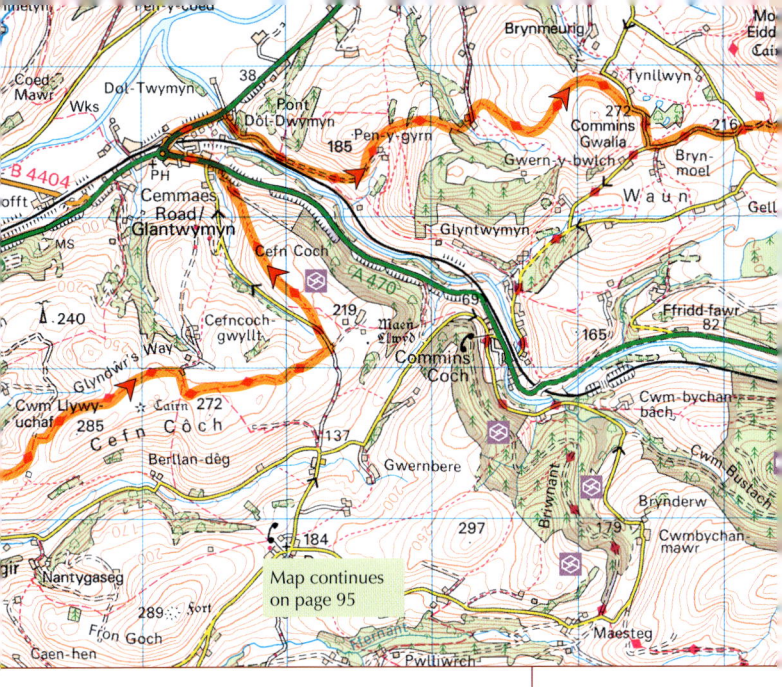

spot a couple of marker posts with yellow plastic caps. Go through another small gate and turn left down a grassy track, passing some rusting vintage tractors. Go through a large gate, then turn right and keep left of a house to drop to the **A470** road. Turn left to follow this to a roundabout and main road junction in **Cemmaes Road**. ▸

The fine old house of **Mathafarn** is about 2km (1¼ miles) off-route from Cemmaes Road, across the Afon Dyfi. Mathafarn has a long history and was visited by Owain Glyndŵr on occasion. Henry VII also visited on his way to fight at Bosworth Field in 1485. He asked the householder, Dafydd Llwyd, whether he would win the battle. Llwyd consulted his wife, who advised him to tell the king he would win – and if the king didn't win, he wouldn't be likely to return and argue about it! A later property was built on the same site by Rowland Pugh in

The Dovey Valley Hotel and a post office shop are available. Buses run back to Machynlleth and ahead to Llanbrynmair, except Sundays.

1628, which was destroyed by Cromwellian forces in 1644. The current building replaced it.

Turn right along the main A470 road as signposted for Welshpool, and walk along the grassy verge on the right, for safety. The road crosses the Afon Twymyn at **Pont Dôl-Dwymyn**, around 40m (130ft). ◄ Turn right through a gate and follow a track that soon rises from the riverside, through another gate. Continue ahead, and a signpost later points straight ahead up the track, where a lesser track forks right. Climb, and a marker post later points left up a steep grassy track on the slopes of **Pen-y-gyrn**. Go down into a dip, then climb steeply through a gate. Climb further, passing a marker post, up through another gate. Go down a short way through yet another gate and walk down a grassy track. Go through a gate and turn left to climb to a farm.

> The road continues 2km (1¼ miles) to Cemmaes, where the Penrhos Arms offers accommodation.

Turn left up the access road, then almost immediately turn right as marked through a gate, and right again to follow a track. The track later turns right, passing through gates from field to field. Turn left uphill, and when the track expires at a higher gate continue along the line of a fence over a rise above 240m (790ft). Go down through another gate, and a grassy track descends gently across a slope of bracken, later passing trees. A gate leads onto a road, where a right turn leads, in effect, straight ahead. Follow the road until it reaches a prominent right-hand bend, and turn left instead down a track. Turn left again, in effect straight ahead up another track, to avoid the farm of **Brynmoel**. Follow the track down to a gate and reach a road.

Turn left up the road, then right as signposted along a track. Follow the grassy track uphill, turning right and left as marked, following a fence onwards. There are fine valley views, with glimpses of southern Eryri and Pumlumon. The track follows an overgrown hawthorn hedge across a slope, generally rising gently, and passes through a wood above the farm of **Fron-gôch**. Climb a bit more steeply and go through a small gate into Gwern-y-bwlch Forest, where there has been a lot of clear-felling and replanting.

Day 6 – Machynlleth to Llanbrynmair

Climb a little, then quickly head down a grassy track to a bend on a gravel track. Turn left as marked up this, and towards the top there is a clear view to the right. Turn right as marked down a short path and go through a small gate to leave the forest. ▶ Turn right and go through a large gate, then cross a squelchy gap and walk up a rushy slope alongside the forest, passing a hill-top marker post at almost 400m (1310ft). Descend alongside the fence, go through a gate, and the forest alongside peters out.

When a marker post suggests veering left, head across boggy ground towards the only gate in view, go through it and follow a grassy path down a firm slope towards a prominent communication mast. Continue straight down a track, through a gate, and past farm machinery to reach a concrete farm road beside big buildings at **Brynaere**, around 200m (655ft). Join the road and pass to the right of the big building. Continue down through the fields, through gates, and turn left as marked to cross a footbridge over a little stream. Continue ahead

There is a view of a wind farm stretching along the top of Mynydd y Cemmaes.

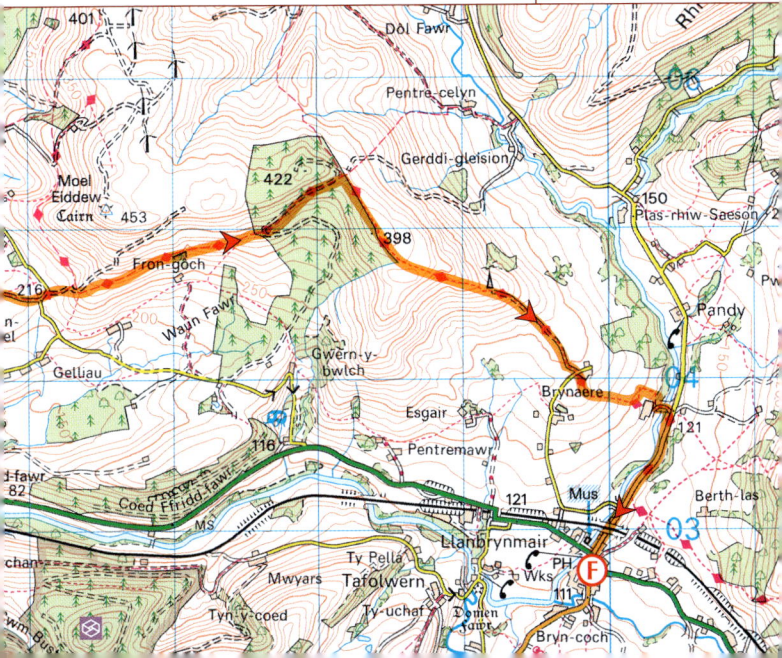

GLYNDŴR'S WAY

The river of Nant-Carfan is seen briefly from a bridge near the farm of Clegyrddwr

alongside a field, until a marked right turn leads towards trees. Turn right again, linking with a track that drops steeply to a farm access road at Clegyrddwr. Turn left to cross a bridge over the Nant-Carfan (Afon Rhiwsaeson on 1:25,000 map), then turn right along and gently down a minor road.

LLANBRYNMAIR

Samuel Roberts, or 'SR' for short, was a 19th-century Congregational minister who was appalled at the ill-treatment of tenants and labourers by greedy landowners around Llanbrynmair. He encouraged many to emigrate to America, with a view to establishing a Welsh colony in Tennessee. In 1857 he was able to write: 'Of all the people born in Llanbrynmair in the last fifty years, there are more now living in America than Llanbrynmair.' Unfortunately, a scheme set up by Roberts to resettle his followers and provide them with employment ultimately failed, due to property and financial disputes. The scheme was finally terminated by the onset of the American Civil War.

Services offered in the village include the Wynnstay Arms Hotel and Wynnstay House B&B. The Wynnstay Stores and Caffi JoJo offer food and drink. There is a campsite with camping pods south of the village at Cringoed. Timberkits (www.timberkits.com), which designs wooden mechanical model kits, has been operating from Llanbrynmair since 1993. There are daily bus services, except Sundays, linking Llanbrynmair with Machynlleth, Penegoes, Cemmaes Road and Newtown.

The road runs parallel to the river, and eventually a signpost points left for Glyndŵr's Way, through a kissing gate into a field. However, looking straight ahead along a road, a railway bridge is seen. Pass beneath this to reach the village of **Llanbrynmair**, which is only 500m off-route, around 100m (330ft).

DAY 7
Llanbrynmair to Llanwddyn

Start	Wynnstay Arms, Llanbrynmair
Finish	Llanwddyn
Distance	29.5km (18½ miles)
Ascent	840m (2755ft)
Descent	690m (2265ft)
Time	9hr
Terrain	Hill pasture, forest, open moorland, broad valleys, farmland, more extensive forest and a reservoir
Maps	OS Landranger 125, 136
Refreshment	Wynnstay Arms Hotel and Caffi JoJo at Llanbrynmair. Cann Office Hotel and Cwpan Pinc café at Llangadfan. Artisans café at Llanwddyn.
Transport	Buses link Llanbrynmair with Machynlleth and Newtown daily, except Sundays. Occasional daily buses, except Sundays, link Llangadfan and Welshpool. Llanwddyn has a Wednesday-only dial-a-ride service to and from Oswestry, which has to be pre-booked.

A fine grassy crest is followed, high above Llanbrynmair, which leads to a forested area high on Panylau Gwynion. After an easy road walk through the broad valley of Nant yr Eira, the route crosses the boggy slopes of Pen Coed. Accommodation, food and drink are available at the crossroads village of Llangadfan, if an early break is required. The extensive plantations of Dyfnant Forest lie ahead, with a couple of scenic breaks. The mighty stone dam of Llyn Efyrnwy is seen at the end of the day, over which spills a cascade of white water when the reservoir is full. This is a popular bird-watching area, where the RSPB operate a visitor centre and bird hides.

Leave **Llanbrynmair** from the Wynnstay Arms Hotel, where the minor road alongside is signposted for Pandy. Follow the road under a railway bridge and keep straight ahead at a junction. A signpost for Glyndŵr's Way points

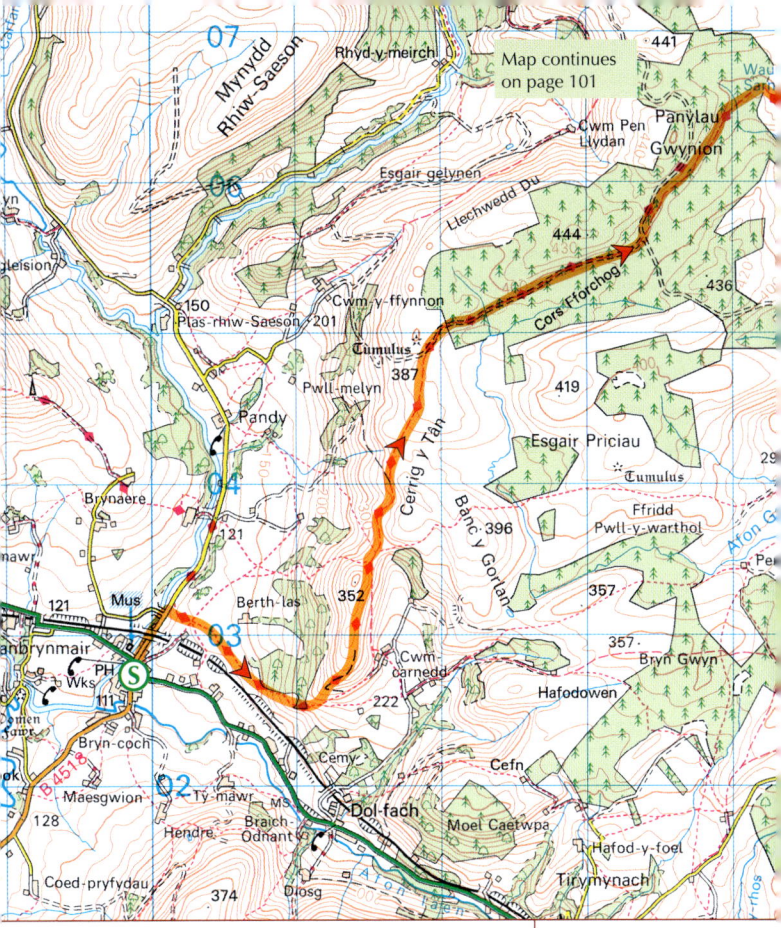

right, through a kissing gate. Walk up a stony track, through a gate and straight ahead at a junction, but quickly step right through a small gate into a field, keeping away from the nearby farm of **Berth-las**. Bear slightly left to cross this rushy field. Aim for the only gates in view, then look to the right to spot a small gate hidden among trees. Go through this into the next field, follow the rampant hedge and fence straight ahead, and cross a footbridge into the next field.

A pool sits in a small quarry on the way down from Panylau Gwynion to the valley of Nant yr Eira

Aim for the far, upper part of the field, where there is a small gate at the corner of a wood. Go through it and climb beside the wood, but watch for marker posts pointing right across the field, then left up a grassy track. Follow the track uphill, through a gate, then further uphill as a grassy ribbon flanked by gorse bushes. Watch for marker posts pointing left and right, taking the route up onto a grassy crest, where there is a tumbled wall and fence, around 280m (920ft). There is a fine view back to the valley, with Llanbrynmair sitting at the heart of it.

Follow the wall and fence uphill a short way, then drift away from them across the grassy slope. Rise to the corner of a fence and the remains of a hawthorn hedge, and later cross a stile beside a gate above **Cwm-carnedd**. Follow a vague path across a slope of thistles, then cross a stile into another area of thistles. Cross a stile beside a gate, in a wall and fence, on a broad grassy gap around 330m (1080ft). The path ahead is much more obvious, cut into the left-hand flank of the grassy hillside of **Cerrig y Tân**. Follow it, rising gently, and pass a junction with another path rising from the left. Join a track on a bend and keep right to go through a gate.

Day 7 – Llanbrynmair to Llanwddyn

The track is plain and obvious as it rises gently on a grassy slope. However, watch for a marker post pointing left later for a small gate at a junction of fences. Go through the gate and follow a fence, then go through another small gate and join a grassy track. Turn right to follow it through a gate into a clear-felled forest at **Cors Fforchog**. Simply walk along and gently up the forest track, and turn left at a junction, around 400m (1310ft). As well as the intentionally planted conifers, note the other self-seeded trees and shrubs, which grow because sheep cannot graze them – willow, rowan, heather and bilberry. Follow the track gently uphill to another marked junction at **Panylau Gwynion**, and turn right downhill along another track. It can get muddy, and after crossing a culverted stream, it is always wet and boggy at **Waun y Sarn**. Rise and go through a small gate in a fence to leave the forest.

Look ahead to spot short marker posts on a boggy moorland slope, which lead up to a fence, around 410m (1345ft). Turn right to walk alongside the fence, and when a gate is reached switch to the other side to continue ahead. Rise gently and go through a small gate at a fence junction, and follow the fence when it later swings left and descends to a marker post at the top end of a track. Follow the track down past a couple of small quarries, down through gates, and reach a minor road in the broad valley of **Nant yr Eira**, around 270m (885ft).

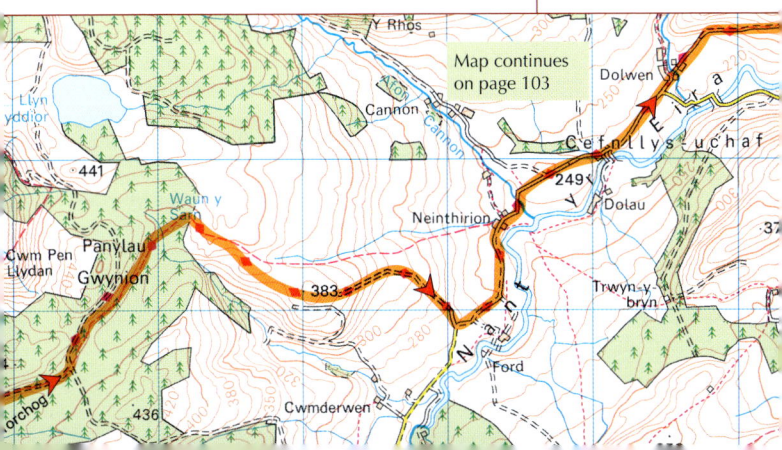

A track climbs from the farm of Dolwen towards the rounded hill of Moel-Ddolwen

Turn left to go along and gently down the road, passing a house, chapel and Victorian post box at **Neinthirion**. Follow the winding road across the **Afon Cannon**, later passing close to the Afon Gam, near the farm access road for **Dolau**. When a triangular road junction is reached, head left (in effect straight ahead) for the farm buildings at **Dolwen**, around 230m (755ft). When the farm is reached, cross a footbridge and walk straight through the farmyard to pick up a grassy track heading for higher ground beyond. The track is muddy at first, then stony as it climbs through gates, flanked by old hawthorn trees. At a higher level, go through a gate and swing left up a clearer track, which bends and reaches a gap near a rounded grassy hill. This is **Moel-Ddolwen**, which is crowned by a hill fort.

Go through another gate, and the track winds uphill, through yet another gate, onto a moorland slope around 320m (1050ft). Follow yellow-topped marker posts ahead, past rushes and gorse, where there are lots of boggy patches. Firmer ground is reached on the rocky hump of Craig Wen, on the shoulder of **Pen Coed**. Keep an eye on the marker posts to descend on drier slopes of bracken and gorse, which become wet and boggy later.

DAY 7 – LLANBRYNMAIR TO LLANWDDYN

The marker posts lead down to a fence, then to a footbridge over the **Nant Nodwydd**, around 220m (720ft).

Turn right as marked, then quickly turn left along a muddy, cow-trodden track up through a gateway into a field. Climb diagonally left uphill, passing a marker post, then look ahead to spot a gate leading into another field, keeping away from the buildings at **Bryn-derwen**. Head for a gate to get onto a minor road, then turn left down the road. Turn left again when a stile appears, and walk down through a little field, into a wood, and leave via a footbridge. Cross a squelchy field and ford a stream, then head for a stile to get onto another minor road.

Turn left up the road, then turn right through a gate and follow a farm access road. Go through a gate at the buildings at **Bryncyrch**, then turn left at a junction and follow the road to another junction, where there are a few houses. Turn right and follow the road to yet another junction, where a marker post points left along a very

short road. In fact, it indicates a footbridge spanning the **Afon Banwy**. After crossing it, rise quickly from one chapel to another, reaching a crossroads on the A458 in the tiny village of **Llangadfan**, around 170m (560ft).

> **Llangadfan** is named after the Breton St Cadfan, who travelled to Wales. It is the only place where this long day's walk can be broken with ease. Just off the crossroads is the Cwpan Pinc tea room and post office shop, while further away, but in plain sight, is the Cann Office Hotel, which offers food, drink, accommodation and an ATM. The Riverbend Caravan Park allows camping. There are occasional daily buses, except Sundays, linking with Welshpool.
>
> The hotel's curious name, 'Cann Office', has nothing to do with an 'office', nor has the date of 1310 over the entrance anything to do with the age of the actual building. In fact, the site was originally occupied by an ancient defensive earthwork or 'foss'. A tenant's name was recorded in 1310 as Madoc ap Owen de Blowty. The placename has been variously rendered as 'Cae'n y ffos' and 'Caen-y-Foss', apparently becoming 'Cann Office' around 1795.

If not stopping in the village, simply cross the main road and continue straight ahead along a minor road. Note a wooden wedge-shaped house to the left. Walk up the road, then down a little, and turn left along the farm access track for **Blowty**. Turn right across a stile into a field, cross to the other side, then turn left to follow the hedgerow up to another stile. Cross this and look straight up a field to spot two prominent trees. The next stile to cross is well to the right of these, then a grassy track is crossed before another stile leads into another field. Walk up through a field, passing a telegraph pole, to find the next stile. Cross over, then walk up through a narrow field and cross yet another stile. Walk straight ahead, then downhill alongside a hedge, to cross a stile

DAY 7 – LLANBRYNMAIR TO LLANWDDYN

and footbridge at the bottom. A short, steep climb and a final stile lead onto a minor road.

Walk straight up the road, which bends left and reaches a junction. Go straight ahead past a gate and stile, then go through a gate and head down across a wet and muddy dip. Rise from this and go through a gate, then follow a grassy track. This gets very wet and muddy, so most walkers pick a parallel course, finally passing to the left of a house at **Penyfford**. A gate leads onto the B4395 road, around 280m (920ft), and just to the left a path leaves the road and enters the first part of an extensive forest.

GLYNDŴR'S WAY

Follow the grassy path uphill and keep right as marked at a junction. Although it may be muddy underfoot, the path soon links with a firm forest track. Turn left to follow it, and it bends right and rises. Keep straight ahead at a track junction, and a good undulating stretch of the track has forest to the left and grassy hills to the right at **Pren Croes**. The track leads back into **Dyfnant Forest**, reaching a complex five-way junction of tracks around 330m (1080ft), where there is an abundance of waymarked routes. The main track runs straight ahead and downhill, while the next track to the right is marked as Glyndŵr's Way and rises very slightly.

An intricate network of colour-coded waymarked trails, featuring numbered junctions, has been established in Dyfnant Forest. The **Rainbow Trails** were developed by the Forestry Commission in partnership with the Dyfnant and Vyrnwy Horse

Glyndŵr's Way descends through an old woodland that pre-dates Dyfnant Forest

Riders and Carriage Drivers Association. As a result, walkers should expect to encounter horse riders and carriage drivers, and should also be aware that bicycles, motorcycles and other vehicles are permitted on some of the forest tracks. Hopefully, all other users will also be on the lookout for walkers! A detailed map of the Rainbow Trails is available online at **rainbowtrails.org.uk/trails-maps**.

The track followed by Glyndŵr's Way runs down to another complex five-way junction of tracks. This time, keep ahead along the track where the greatest distance can be seen downhill. On the way down the track, step to the left as marked down a more rugged track. This runs parallel to a stream in a ravine, where tall oaks and sycamores pre-date the forest plantation. Cross a bend on another track and go straight down through a gate as marked. Follow a track beside a grassy area, with views

GLYNDŵR'S WAY

down a valley. The track rises among trees, then reaches a stream. Believe it or not, walkers are supposed to hobble downstream along the streambed, then cross a footbridge over another stream, around 250m (820ft).

Follow a track and turn right as signposted at a nearby track junction, heading gently downhill. The track is actually a narrow tarmac road, but often battered, broken and strewn with stones. It rises and falls on the slopes of **Moel Achles**, with mature forest to the left and usually oaks to the right, along with occasional views down the valley. Reach a road junction and continue straight ahead. The road rises, and even climbs steeply at one point, then it descends and passes the entrance to a caravan park at **Ddôl Cownwy**, around 220m (720ft).

Cross a bridge over the Afon Cownwy, turning left and left again at road junctions very close together. Soon afterwards, turn right up a track as signposted. ◀ Walk up the track and keep straight ahead at a triangular junction, then before reaching **Bryn Cownwy** turn right at a junction where there is a white gate and climb steeply. Watch carefully on the left to spot a fenced memorial stone marking an old Quaker burial ground.

Keeping straight ahead along the minor road leads to a B&B at Penisarcwm.

Day 7 – Llanbrynmair to Llanwddyn

The Lake Vyrnwy Hotel and Spa offers upmarket accommodation off-route across the dam

Keep straight ahead as marked at a track junction, climbing at a gentler gradient. Cross a forested crest, around 350m (1150ft), turn left and descend gently to a track intersection, where there is a glimpse of the Vyrnwy Reservoir and the Vyrnwy Hotel. Walk straight ahead and immediately turn right to cross a stile beside a gate. Drop beside the woodland fence, where it can be wet and muddy, and follow a duckboard to a stile at the bottom. Turn right to another stile and gate, then go straight ahead down a track with more views of the reservoir dam. Reach buildings, a road and a Glyndŵr's Way signpost at **Llanwddyn**, around 250m (820ft).

GLYNDŴR'S WAY

LLANWDDYN AND LLYN EFYRNWY

Water spills over the monumental stone dam of Llyn Efyrnwy, or Lake Vyrnwy

Llyn Efyrnwy (Lake Vyrnwy) is an impressive Victorian reservoir with a stone dam, constructed to supply the distant city of Liverpool with clean water. When the reservoir was constructed, the village of Llanwddyn was drowned, with the loss of 37 houses, 10 farmhouses, three inns and two chapels. Remnants of the village appear when the water level is low. By way of compensation, two new villages were constructed – one close to the dam, with a church, and the other down in the valley.

Llyn Efyrnwy's statistics can be compared with Llyn Clywedog on Day 4:
- Height of dam spillway: 44m (144ft)
- Length of dam: 357m (1171ft)
- Maximum depth of water: 25m (82ft)
- Level of spillway: 252m (827ft) above sea level
- Volume of water impounded: 59,665 million litres (13,125 million gallons)
- Surface area: 2455 hectares (1125 acres)
- Length of reservoir: 7.5km (4½ miles)
- Direct catchment area: 74km^2 (28½ square miles)
- Indirect additional catchment area: 21km^2 (8 square miles)
- Construction commenced: 25 Oct 1882
- Impounding commenced: 26 Nov 1888

> There is accommodation at Dam View Cottage at Llanwyddyn, with the Lake Vyrnwy Hotel lying on the other side of the reservoir. Also available is the Artisans café, offering bicycle hire for anyone who wants to add a 19km (12-mile) circuit of the B4393 road around the reservoir. There are two visitor centres – one is dedicated to the reservoir; the other is operated by the RSPB (www.rspb.org.uk), which also provides a bird-watching hide nearby. Despite the popularity of the area, the only transport available is a Wednesday-only dial-a-ride service to and from Oswestry, which has to be pre-booked.

Towards the end of this stage of the walk, signposts and waymarks will be seen for the **Pererindod Melangell Walk**, which stretches 24km (15 miles) from Pont Llogel to Llanwddyn, then over the hills to St Melangell's Church and Llangynog. According to legend, a seventh-century prince named Brochwel was hunting around Pennant, near Llangynog, when his dogs put a hare to flight. He gave chase and found a virgin, Melangell, at prayer, with the hare hidden in the folds of her cloak. The dogs fled the scene, and Melangell explained that she sought refuge in this remote area. Brochwel was overcome by her piety and granted her land for the foundation of a nunnery.

GLYNDŴR'S WAY

DAY 8
Llanwddyn to Meifod

Start	Llanwddyn
Finish	Meifod
Distance	24.5km (15¼ miles)
Ascent	445m (1460ft)
Descent	610m (2000ft)
Time	8hr
Terrain	Valley and riverside walking, with woodland, farmland and forest, as well as occasional hills
Maps	OS Landranger 125
Refreshment	Artisans café at Llanwddyn. Shop at Abertridwr. Shop at Pont Llogel. Royal Oak Hotel at Pontrobert. Kings Head Hotel at Meifod.
Transport	A Monday-only bus links Llwydiarth with Welshpool. A Monday-only bus links Dolanog and Pontrobert with Welshpool. Wednesday and Friday buses link Pontrobert and Meifod with Oswestry. Buses connect Meifod and Welshpool daily, except Sundays.

A cursory glance at a map suggests that this entire stage follows the Afon Efyrnwy downstream. However, the route runs beside the river only on a couple of occasions, crosses it three times, and generally keeps its distance from the flow. Nearby hills are crossed, notably Allt Dolanog, and there are a succession of ascents and descents. Signposts for the Ann Griffiths Walk will be seen in some places, where it crosses Glyndŵr's Way or enjoys a stretch in common – notably at Pont Llogel, Dolanog and Pontrobert. This stage finishes at Meifod, at the lowest point on the route since Machynlleth.

Leave **Llanwddyn** by walking down a minor road, past the last few houses, and into woods. Keep right at a road junction as marked, then continue through the woods to another road junction and keep left. When the road comes close to buildings, turn left as signposted through a gate and follow a track downhill. When a building is reached, go through a gate and climb to another gate

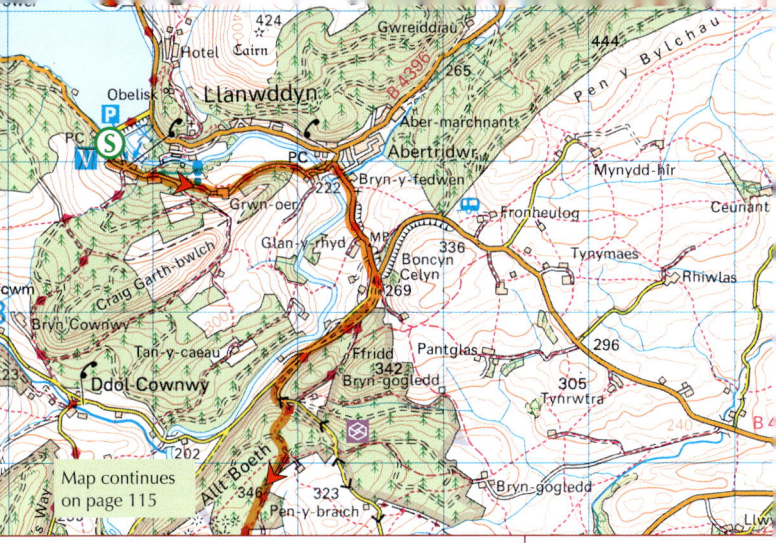

to the left of a house called **Grwn-oer**. Go through the gate and descend beneath the boughs of two huge horse chestnut trees. The track continues through a couple more gates and reaches a junction. Turn left to cross a bridge over the Afon Efyrnwy and reach the B4393 road at **Abertridwr**, at 222m (728ft). ▶

There is a shop up to the left.

Turn right to follow the road away from the village, up to a sharp bend and road junction on the slopes of **Boncyn Celyn**. ▶ Continue straight ahead as signposted for Cownwy, down a minor road. Turn left when a forest track leaves the road, following it uphill and crossing a forested gap at almost 300m (985ft). Keep straight ahead downhill from a junction. ▶ When the track joins a minor road, turn right uphill, then left as signposted up another nearby track. Turn right up an impressive flight of 169 wooden steps. A grassy path continues up between trees, joining a forest track on **Yr Allt Boeth**, around 330m (1080ft).

An occasional campsite is available close to the river, opposite Bryn-y-fedwen.

A diversion might be in place, heading straight down the road to Pont Llogel.

Turn left to follow the track, then turn right at a junction. The track runs downhill, but watch on the right for a marker post revealing a path climbing back uphill. Cross a stile and leave the forest, heading for a marker post ahead. Continue down beyond it and cross a stile into a forest. Walk down a grassy path, steep and narrow at

The route passes within sight of a little cottage, Parc-bach, near Pont Llogel

times, brushing against trees, then cross a stile at the bottom. Turn right alongside the fence and continue down short flights of wooden steps, later squeezing past gorse bushes beside the fence. Reach a gate and stile and turn right down a grassy track into forest at **The Warren**. Turn left as marked along a path, which later climbs from a marker post and reaches a small gate beside an old quarry, leaving the wood.

There is a view of a little house called Parc-bach, but keep away from it and walk straight ahead, watching for a marker post showing the way to a gate and stile. It can be wet underfoot around here, so keep to firmer

Day 8 – Llanwddyn to Meifod

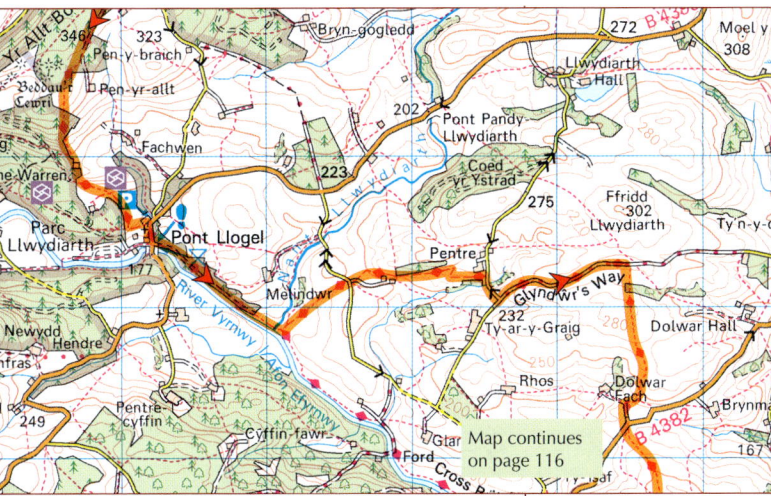

footing while walking past tall oak trees to reach a gate overlooking a caravan park. Go through the gate and turn left, where it can be wet and muddy, and go through a couple more gates to pass a church and rebuilt schoolhouse. Then follow a track down to the B4395 road at **Pont Llogel**, around 180m (590ft). ▶

There is a post office shop in view, just up the road.

Turn right to walk down the road to the actual bridge called Pont Llogel, but don't cross it. Turn left as signposted into a forest car park, and follow a clear, well-wooded, gravel riverside path beside the **Afon Efyrnwy**. This passes rockfaces from time to time. Go through a gate and continue through a field, crossing a footbridge over a tributary called **Nant Llwydiarth**. Turn left up through a field, following an even smaller stream. At the top of the field, cross to the other side at a gate and keep walking upstream. Cross a stile to see where a spring feeds the stream, then continue up through the field, alongside a rampant hedge, to a gate and a minor road.

Walk along the farm access road towards Llwynhir, but soon turn left through a gate into a field. Pass to the left of the farm buildings, go through a gate and walk up

GLYNDŴR'S WAY

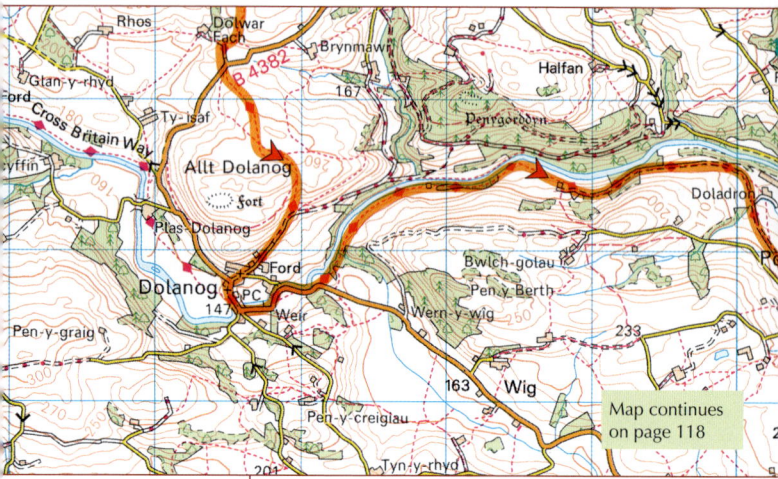

a grassy track beside a forest. Leave via a small gate at the top, then turn right downhill and soon turn left to pass below the farm of **Pentre** and go through a small gate. Turn right down the road, up over a crest, then turn left as signposted up through a gate onto a track.

Follow the track, which is flanked by old hawthorn hedges, with occasional big oak trees. Go through another gate, with the trees alongside very tangled, continuing on the slopes of **Fridd Llwydiarth**. Watch for a gate and stile on the right, where a couple of marker posts point right. Here turn right and walk down into a dip, then up across a stile. Follow a fence uphill, over a rise around 280m (920ft), then go down to cross another stile. Follow the fence straight ahead to cross another stile, then turn right and follow a fence to cross yet another stile. Turn left to follow a fence to a marker post, then turn right downhill to cross a stile onto a farm road near **Dolwar Fach**. Turn left to walk up to a triangular road junction and turn right as signposted. Just a short way along the road, turn left as signposted, where there is a gate and a stile, as well as a stone tablet commemorating the Ann Griffiths Walk.

Day 8 – Llanwddyn to Meifod

Go straight up a grassy, rushy slope, watching for marker posts. These indicate where the path veers right, then turns left, reaching a rocky outcrop around 270m (885ft) near the top of **Allt Dolanog**. ▶ Enjoy views of the surrounding countryside, which is all hills and valleys, without any particular distinguishing features. Walk downhill as marked, picking up a clear path crossing a footbridge and joining a track further down. Turn right gently down the track, going through a gate, and it becomes a road leading past the Ann Griffiths Memorial Chapel. Note the bronze 'book' sculpture, then keep straight ahead downhill, reaching a junction on the B4382 road in the middle of **Dolanog**, around 150m (490ft). ▶

Certain areas of bracken are managed to conserve two rare butterfly species – the high-brown and pearl-bordered fritillaries.

The road to the right leads to the Camp Plas campsite at Plas Dolanog.

ANN GRIFFITHS WALK

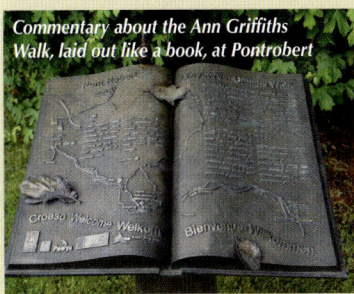

Commentary about the Ann Griffiths Walk, laid out like a book, at Pontrobert

Ann Thomas was born in 1776 at Dolwar Fach and went to school at nearby Llanfihangel-yng-Ngwynfa. Her entire life was spent in this area, and she never travelled further than Bala, where she heard sermons delivered by the Methodist preacher Thomas Charles. Ann was inspired to compose hymns in her native Welsh language, which were committed to memory by a maid at Dolwar Fach, Ruth Hughes. Ann married Thomas Griffiths of Meifod, but died in childbirth in 1805 and was buried at Llanfihangel-yng-Ngwynfa. Ruth married the preacher John Hughes of Pontrobert, and he wrote down Ann's hymns and had them published in 1806.

The Ann Griffiths Walk is signposted and waymarked, but also equipped with splendid bronze sculptures in the form of open 'books', wonderfully crafted with route descriptions and notes about local lore and wildlife. The Ann Griffiths Walk measures 11.5km (7 miles). It criss-crosses or runs concurrent with Glyndŵr's Way at Pont Llogel, Dolanog and Pontrobert. Either route can be followed between the three villages if desired.

Old stepping stones can be seen crossing the Afon Efyrnwy on the way out of Dolanog

Turn left to walk up the road, past the war memorial and St John's Church, then continue down to cross an old bridge beside the modern road bridge spanning the **Afon Efyrnwy**. The B4382 road runs close to the river, but trees often screen views. However, a weir might be seen through foliage, followed by a set of old stepping stones that once served a farm. When the road climbs, watch for a stile on the left. Walk straight across a field and cross another stile. The path stays above the river, often

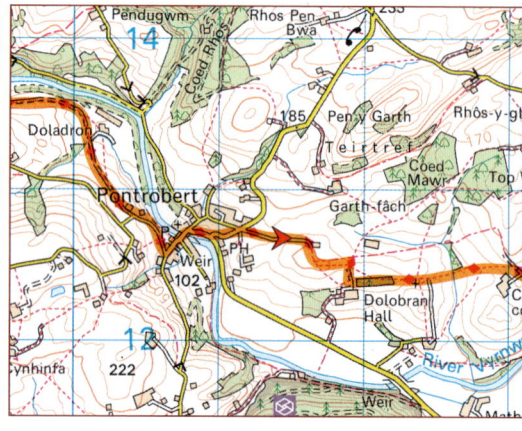

Day 8 – Llanwddyn to Meifod

wooded, with glimpses of rocks in the riverbed and on nearby slopes. There are some grassy stretches with occasional stiles, and an old cottage is passed. One wooded stretch can be muddy, then a gate gives access to a track.

The track climbs towards a gate near a house. Step to the left to follow a hedge past the house, then use a small gate to get back onto the access track. Turn left to follow the track uphill, crossing a cattle grid, then descend gently into woods. After a gentle rise later, the track becomes a narrow tarmac road. Pass a junction with another road above the farm of **Doladrog**. Climb again, eventually reaching another road junction where eggs might be on sale in a little hut. Turn left downhill, then left again at a school, heading down to a bridge spanning the river at **Pontrobert**, around 100m (330ft).

At **Pontrobert** there is a post office on the right just before the bridge and another bronze 'book'. The John Hughes Memorial Chapel lies off-route and is associated with Ann Griffiths. There are two more chapels and a little church dotted around the village.

Cross the bridge and turn right as signposted for Meifod, following the road across a small river. Turn left

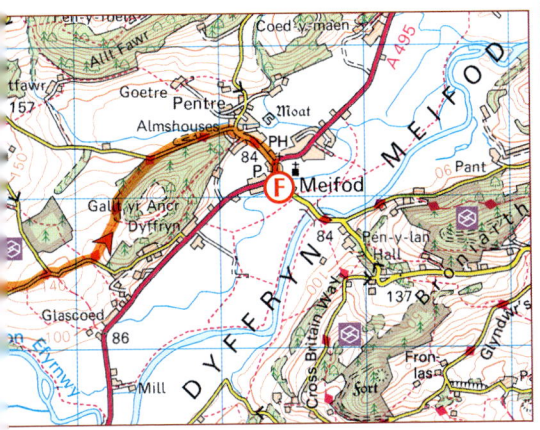

at a roadside chapel, following a road up past the Royal Oak, reaching another roadside chapel. Turn right as signposted along a narrow road, marked as 'no through road'. Walk up this road until the tarmac ends at a house. Turn right to follow a grassy track flanked by hedges, then turn left through a gate, around 150m (490ft). Follow the track downhill and go through another gate, then turn right uphill. At the top of the track, go through a gate on the left, but immediately turn right alongside the field to reach a gate in a corner overlooking **Dolobran Hall**. Don't go through the gate, but turn left to walk beside a wood, noting that the ground is soft and full of holes made by the hooves of cattle.

Go through a small gate and walk straight ahead across and down a field. ◄ Marker posts link with a grassy track flanked by hedges. Go down this, then turn right along another track, going through a gate and up through a field. Don't leave this field, but turn left to go up through a small gate in its top corner. Walk straight ahead to join a track, and turn right to walk down it, well away from the farm of **Coed-cowrhyd**. Continue straight ahead down a road. At the bottom of the road, cross a stile beside a gate and walk straight up through a field towards trees on the skyline. Another stile leads back onto the road.

Look out to the right to spot an old Quaker Meeting House.

A track descends from a field to a road near the farm of Coed-cowrhyd

DAY 8 – LLANWDDYN TO MEIFOD

Turn left to follow the road to a junction, and keep straight ahead downhill. Watch for a footpath signpost pointing left, but stay on the road for a little longer to spot a Glyndŵr's Way signpost pointing left through a small gate. Follow a muddy track uphill, then head down to a marker post and continue down to the bottom of the field to find a gate and a muddy track leading into a wood on the lower slopes of **Gallt yr Ancr**. ▶ The track rises and falls, later going through a gate onto a minor road. Turn right to follow the road, which later drops to a junction among houses at **Pentre**. ▶ Turn right to follow the road, passing a school, to reach a junction on the A495 road in **Meifod**, at 84m (275ft).

Gallt yr Ancr is named after an anchorite's cell on the hill, possibly belonging to Gwyddfarch.

Turn left to reach a basic campsite nearby at Pentrego Farm.

MEIFOD

The King's Head pub

This unassuming village was once a centre of state and church power. The first church was founded by Gwyddfarch in the sixth century. One story says that when Gwyddfarch was asked where he wanted to build his church, he answered 'Yma y mae i fod' or 'Here it is to be'. The Princes of Powys were based at nearby Mathrafal from the ninth century until 1212, when their fort was destroyed during a conflict with Llywelyn ap Iorwerth of Gwynedd. Prince Gwenwynwyn ap Owain took this opportunity to re-establish his fort on an elevated site near Welshpool, now occupied by Powis Castle. The churchyard of St Tysilio & St Mary at Meifod is huge, and was the burial place of some of the early Princes of Powys.

The village has a post office shop and the King's Head Hotel offers meals, accommodation and a campsite. Tan y Graig B&B lies outside the village, but will provide pick-ups and drop-offs.

DAY 9
Meifod to Welshpool

Start	Meifod
Finish	Howell Park, Welshpool
Distance	18km (11 miles)
Ascent	550m (1805ft)
Descent	565m (1855ft)
Time	5hr 30mins
Terrain	Valleys, farmland and woodland, leading to an open hill top
Maps	OS Landranger 125, 126
Refreshment	King's Head hotel at Meifod. Plenty of choice in Welshpool.
Transport	Buses connect Meifod and Welshpool daily, except Sundays. Welshpool has good rail connections with Aberystwyth, Machynlleth and Shrewsbury, linking with mainline services at Birmingham. Buses link Welshpool with Shrewsbury.

The final stage of Glyndŵr's Way is short, but remarkably convoluted, featuring a succession of small hills. The last hill, Y Golfa, is a splendid viewpoint, allowing views back into the heart of Wales, as well as across the Severn lowlands to Long Mountain, which is traversed by the Offa's Dyke Path. The end of the trail is in the busy market town of Welshpool. Before leaving, a visit to Powis Castle is recommended, where the elevated red sandstone façade overlooks splendid gardens. On the other hand, the journey can continue for two more days along the Offa's Dyke Path (see Days 10 and 11), which links Welshpool with Knighton, thus creating a circular walk that returns walkers to their starting point.

Leave the road junction in the middle of **Meifod**. Walk to a nearby road junction and turn left as signposted for the rugby club. Cross the broad valley floor of **Dyffryn Meifod** and cross a bridge over the Afon Efyrnwy. Turn left at another road junction, along Ffordd Glyndŵr, and

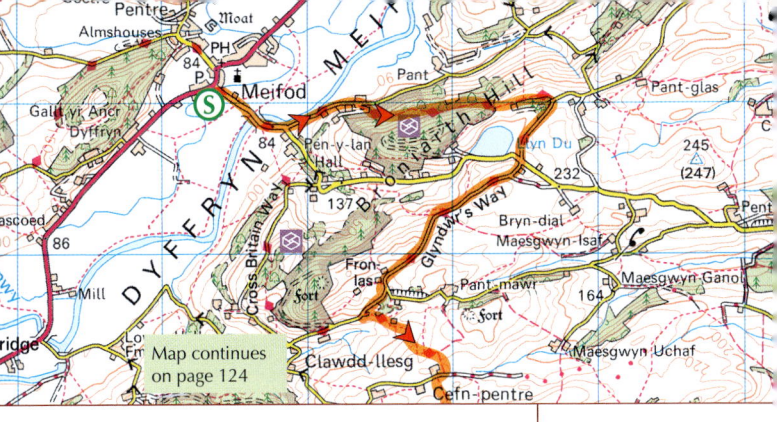

the road climbs, reaching a house called Hillcroft. Fork right and climb up a steep woodland track. When the track bends sharply right, walk straight ahead up a path through mixed woodland. When the path bends sharply right, walk straight ahead again along a grassy path. Go through a small gate and continue through woods until another small gate leads out into a field on **Broniarth Hill**.

Walk straight ahead and turn left to walk beside a fence and hedge. There are views of a lake, **Llyn Du**, but keep walking along the full length of the field, around 220m (720ft), to find a gate leading onto a minor road. Turn right to walk down the road, with another view of the lake, then go straight through a crossroads. Climb steeply and pass the black-and-white Bryndial Cottage. The road climbs and later levels out, with views on the right back to Meifod, as well as to distant mountains, including Pumlumon. Cross a crest and follow the road down the other side, eventually reaching a road junction below **Fron-las**.

Turn right as signposted, down beside a wooded valley, then turn left as signposted through a gate. Walk down a path, through another gate, then cross an old dam in the woods. Watch for marker posts while climbing a steep, grassy slope, then walk downhill and pass a ruined brick-and-timber house called Ty-newydd. Go through a gate and follow the fence to the left, climbing to the corner of a field and go through a small gate

A glimpse of Llyn Du from a field on the brow of Broniarth Hill

on the left. Walk to a corner of the field and go through another small gate into another field. Turn right to walk beside this field, and go through two gates to the right of

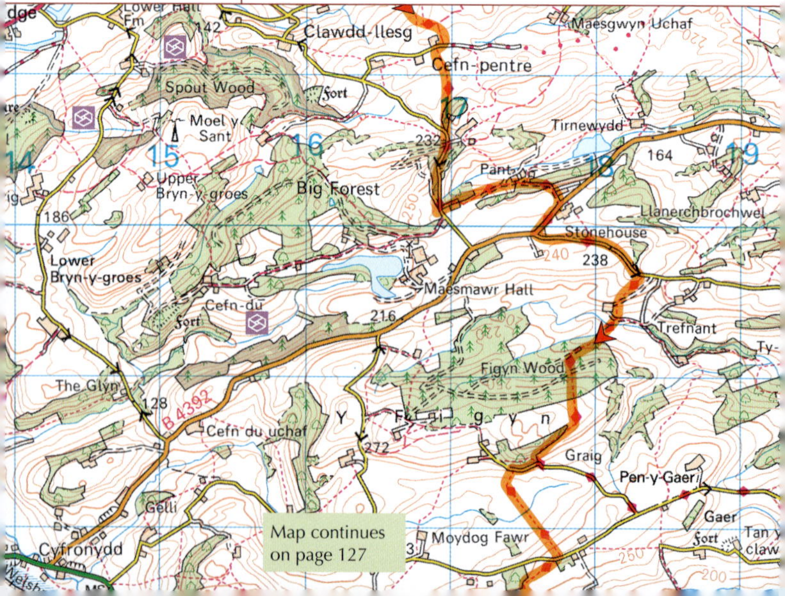

Map continues on page 127

a farm called **Cefn-pentre**. Turn right along a path shaded by trees, emerging onto the farm access road.

Almost immediately, turn left through a small gate, head straight across a field, then continue down among trees to find another gate. Cross a field to find another gate, then head up towards a rounded hill crowned by a wood. A marker post might be spotted; otherwise simply keep right and follow the woodland fence round and down to a gate. Turn left up a road, where there is a Caravan Club site to the left, and cross a wooded gap beside **Big Forest**. Drop steeply along the road, then while walking uphill, watch for a signpost and a small gate on the left. Follow a path to reach a bend on a track and follow the track as it rises gently through a field. The track later descends towards buildings in a valley at **Pant**. ▶

Go through a gate to reach a track junction and walk straight down through another gate onto a road bend. Turn right and climb across a steep beechwood slope, overlooking mobile homes. Turn right at a higher level up to a road junction facing **Stonehouse Farm**. Turn right to follow the road gently uphill, then turn left at a triangular road junction beside The Old School. Follow the road uphill to 238m (780ft), then cross a dip before heading steeply downhill. Watch for a gate on the right, where a signpost indicates a sharp right turn. Don't go through the next gate, but keep left of it as marked. Look ahead across and down a slope to spot other markers, which lead to an access track near a farm at **Trefnant**, around 170m (560ft).

Cross the track and go through a gate, then walk down a field and turn right through a gate onto a track. Leave this to cross a small footbridge and go through a small gate. Turn right along the bottom edge of a field, leaving through another small gate. Follow a narrow path through mixed forest, called **Figyn Wood**. Turn left to climb a couple of flights of wooden steps and keep following the path up through the woods.

Go through a small gate into a field on **Y Figyn**, around 280m (920ft). Head for a stile and cross a fence,

This is also known as the Hidden Valley Holiday Home Park.

The old house called Pant, situated beside the Hidden Valley Holiday Home Park

then head through a gate and walk down a track flanked by bracken. Don't go down into a field, but turn right along a path across a lovely wooded slope above **Graig**, which may have a splendid ground cover of flowers. Go through a small gate, and soon after turn left down a flight of 52 wooden steps to a minor road. Turn right along the road, which goes gently down and up, watching for a signpost and a gate on the left.

Go through the gate and bear right down through a field and go through a small gate. Turn left and walk straight ahead, looking for markers that lead to a gate and a culverted drainage ditch. Climb straight uphill alongside a fence. Drop a little to cross a minor road, using gates on both sides. Bear right across a field, heading for the left corner of a woodland. Reaching the corner, turn left and climb straight towards the hill ahead. This reveals a small gate giving access to a golf course. Turn left to follow markers around the overgrown lower edge of the golf course, then turn right and climb beside a fence.

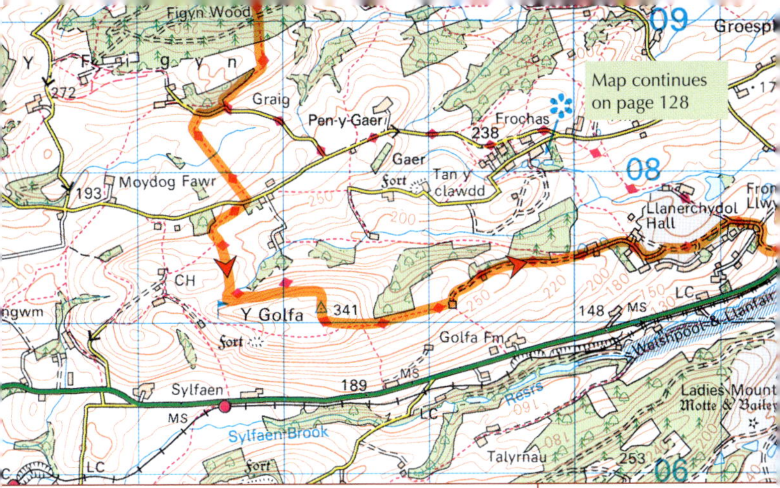

Map continues on page 128

Cross a crest, then head downhill and left, through a boggy patch, to cross a footbridge. Climb to a firm path and turn right as marked. When a path junction is reached, turn left and climb a steep slope of bracken, then bend sharp left. The path runs along a high edge of the golf course, continuing with bracken to the left and gorse bushes to the right. Watch the marker posts,

The view from the summit of Y Golfa, the last hill climbed before Welshpool

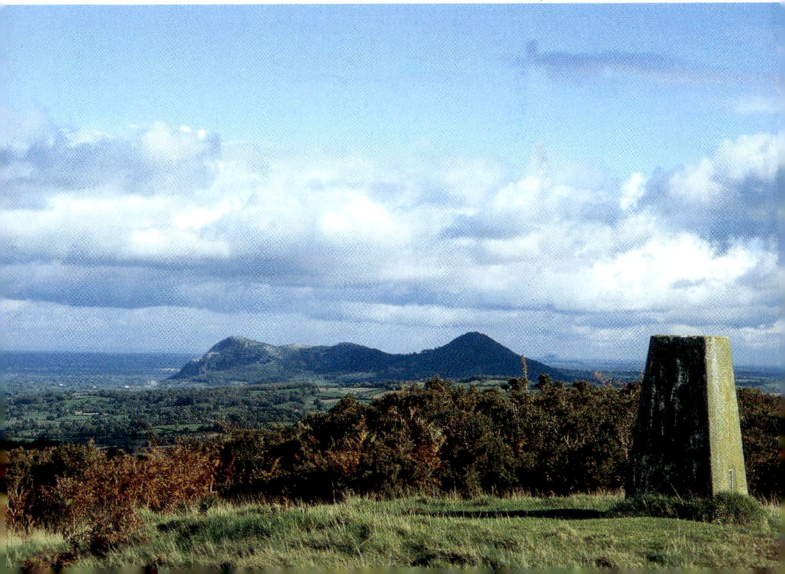

as one of them suddenly indicates a right-hand turn, and the path makes a short, steep climb to a trig point on **Y Golfa**, at 341m (1120ft). Enjoy the last extensive views on Glyndŵr's Way, stretching from the Welsh–English borderlands around Long Mountain, deep into mid-Wales.

The path runs gently down the crest, and more marker posts indicate turnings to right and left, then right and left again. Go through a gate at the corner of a wood, then walk alongside the wood to a gate and stile. Keep walking beside the wood, through a gate, and keep left of a solitary house at 250m (820ft). Follow a track as marked, beneath the boughs of a spreading oak tree. Cross a stile beside a gate near a building and keep walking down the track, later passing houses at Ramblers Barn. Follow the track down through woods and eventually into open parkland, where there are many fine tall trees. Join a tarmac road and follow it past **Llanerchydol Hall** all the way down to a junction of main roads at Raven Square, on the outskirts of **Welshpool**.

WELSHPOOL

During Glyndŵr's rebellion Welshpool, Montgomery and the surrounding countryside were largely controlled by the Welsh, but Powis Castle was garrisoned by the English, who could not be dislodged. Originally, the town was simply called 'Pool', but was changed to 'Welshpool' to avoid confusion with 'Poole' in Dorset. In Welsh, as 'Y Trallwng', there is no confusion. The town was a notable centre

Day 9 – Meifod to Welshpool

for trade in flannels. These days, the Livestock Market hosts one of the largest one-day shows in Europe.

The first feature of interest seen on the outskirts is the Raven Square Station on the steam-hauled Welshpool and Llanfair Light Railway (www.wllr.org.uk). This line opened in 1903 and closed in 1956, but was reopened by railway enthusiasts in 1963. Welshpool town centre features a French Renaissance style Town Hall with an imposing clock tower. There are plenty more old and interesting buildings, some of them charmingly crooked and timber-framed. The first church founded in the area dated from the sixth century. As soon as the town centre is passed, the Montgomery Canal is crossed, where the Powysland Museum is located in the last of 30 warehouses that stood beside the canal in the 19th century (see www.powyslandclub.co.uk).

Welshpool has a full range of facilities, including accommodation, banks, post office, shops, pubs, restaurants and take-aways, including Andrews – 'Voted No1 Fish & Chip Shop in Wales'. A tourist information centre is available on Church Street (tel 01938 552043). There are good rail connections with Shrewsbury and mainline services at Birmingham, while bus services also link with Shrewsbury.

Walk to the far side of a roundabout and pass The Raven Inn to follow a road into town. Raven Street becomes Mount Street, changing to High Street and Broad Street in the town centre. ▶ Simply keep walking straight ahead until the road crosses the Shropshire Union Canal. At this point, look left into the tiny grassy space of Howell Park to see a Glyndŵr's Way commemorative stone, which marks the end of the trail. If you are in a desperate hurry to leave, keep walking straight ahead to reach the railway station, but Welshpool and Powis Castle deserve to be explored. To return to Knighton on foot, follow Days 10 and 11 along Offa's Dyke Path.

Watch for a road on the right signposted for Powis Castle, which is well worth visiting if time can be spared.

The elevated site occupied by **Powis Castle** has a long history of fortification and has long been associated with Welsh royalty. The last hereditary Prince of Powys, Owain ap Gruffydd ap Gwenwynwyn, renounced his title in 1266 and was made Baron de la Pole – as in 'Pool' or 'Welshpool'. One of Owain's descendants sold the lordship and castle

Powis Castle looks across country towards Beacon Ring and Offa's Dyke

to Sir Edward Herbert in the 16th century. The title 'Earl of Powis' has been created three times, in the 17th, 18th and 19th centuries. The Herbert family, in association with the Clive family, have developed the castle over four centuries, and it is now a National Trust property. The castle is also known as Castell Coch ('red castle'), and its ruddy hue is due to the red sandstone used in its construction. The parkland around the castle, where fallow deer can be seen grazing, can be visited free, dawn until dusk. The restaurant in the castle can be visited free during opening hours. The rest of the castle and the gardens have an admission charge, and opening times can be checked on 01938 551944.

DAY 10
Welshpool to Brompton Cross

Start	Howell Park, Welshpool
Finish	Blue Bell Hotel, Brompton Cross
Distance	22.5km (14 miles)
Ascent	420m (1380ft)
Descent	350m (1150ft)
Time	7hr
Terrain	Apart from the ascent and descent of a partly forested hill, most of the route runs through low-lying farmland
Maps	OS Landranger 126, 137
Refreshment	Plenty of choice in Welshpool. Blue Bell Hotel at Brompton Cross. Plenty of choice off-route in Montgomery.
Transport	Welshpool has good rail connections with Aberystwyth, Machynlleth and Shrewsbury, linking with mainline services at Birmingham. Buses link Welshpool, Forden and Montgomery with Shrewsbury.

From Welshpool the route follows Offa's Dyke Path on a two-day return to Knighton. Although the eighth-century Offa's Dyke runs along the foot of Long Mountain, the more recent Offa's Dyke Path climbs to the summit, where an Iron Age hill fort contains a hidden message spelled out by trees. After enjoying views from the rampart of the hill fort, the path is reunited with the Dyke and heads southwards across low-lying farmland around Forden. The pleasant, attractive, interesting little town of Montgomery lies just off-route and offers a small but adequate range of services. Facilities around Brompton Cross, however, are spread thinly throughout the surrounding countryside.

Start at Howell Park in **Welshpool**, where there is an information board for Glyndŵr's Way, as well as a marker stone. Follow a short path to the Montgomery Canal and turn right along the towpath. Lledan Brook is crossed just before the towpath passes under a bridge. Go under a

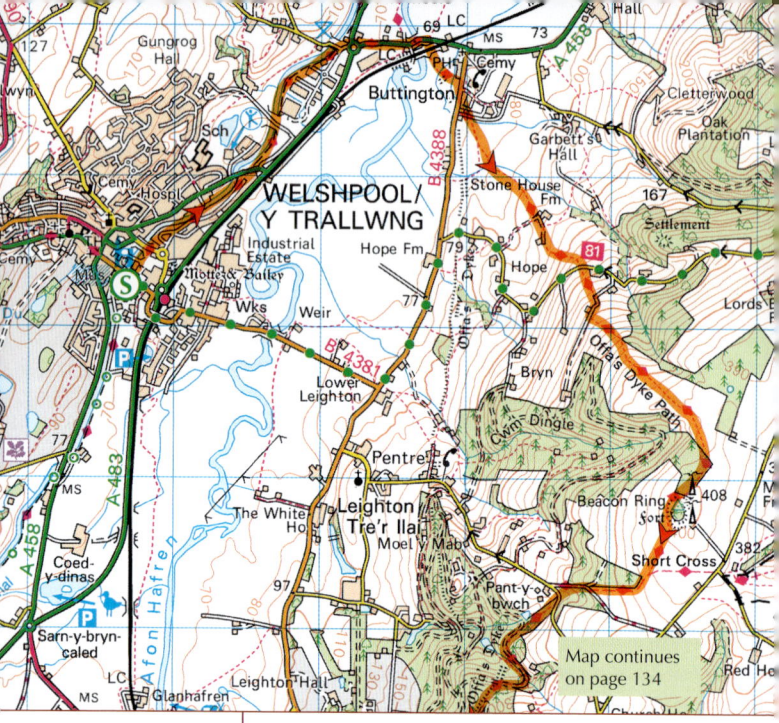

road bridge shortly afterwards and follow the towpath past houses to leave town. Later, the canal has been diverted and is bridged by a busy main road. Follow the course of the old canal and towpath, cross the busy road, then pick up the towpath and follow it out of town.

Go under another bridge and pass Gungrog Wharf, where the 'Heulwen' narrowboats are moored. When the next bridge is reached, number 115, climb steps and turn right along a road. Quickly turn left at a junction to reach a roundabout at Buttington Cross, near the large Livestock Market. Follow the A458 as signposted for Shrewsbury, using the pavement alongside, although there is no pavement while crossing a bridge over the **River Severn**, now following the Offa's Dyke Path.

Turn right along a short field path and cross a railway with care. Go straight through a field, lining up gates

Day 10 – Welshpool to Brompton Cross

and stiles, to reach the B4388 road just to the right of **Buttington**. ▶ Cross the road and turn right along the pavement, then pass the Offa's Dyke Business Park. A wooden palisade stands beside the pavement, and it has been suggested that Offa's Dyke once boasted such a structure. Pass the palisade and turn left as signposted, keeping left of School House. Follow a broad grassy path, and turn right through a gate into a field. Cross two fields, rising gently, then cross a footbridge. Follow a path, a grassy track and a stony track uphill, keeping right of **Stone House Farm**.

Keep following a track uphill to another house. Turn left through a gate as marked, then immediately right up a field path. Climb steeply through a long field, passing occasional tall trees, to reach a road. Cross over to continue climbing through another field, keeping well to the right of a house called Buttington View. Climb through another field, then follow a track that veers right, passing a house. Go through a gate and immediately turn left, straight uphill. Go through another gate and climb diagonally right up through the next field. Go through yet another gate and climb gently beside the next field. Cross

The Green Dragon Inn is on the main road and has a campsite.

Buttington Bridge, outside Welshpool, which is crossed by the Offa's Dyke Path

GLYNDŴR'S WAY

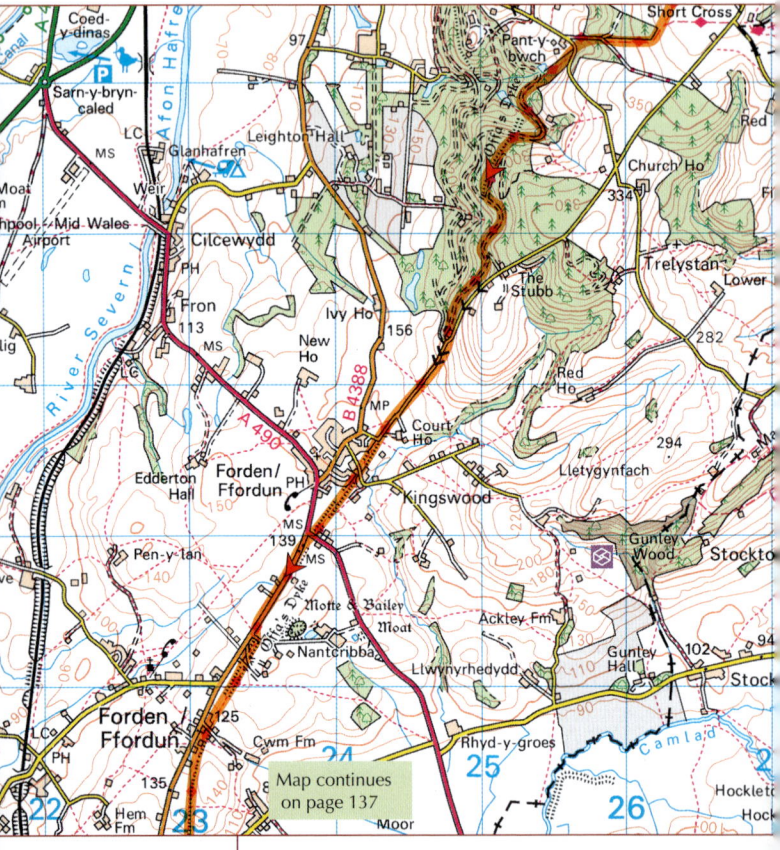

a smaller field with gates at either end, then veer slightly to the right to cross a larger field. Don't follow a track, but look carefully for a barely trodden path, and avoid being drawn near a forest at the head of **Cwm Dingle** until a marker post has been passed.

Go through a gate into the young forest, where the path might be wet. Continue into tall forest, passing close to a communication mast, then cross a stile to reach a small information board about **Beacon Ring**. A

Day 10 – Welshpool to Brompton Cross

beechwood sits inside the circular earth embankment of an Iron Age hill fort, which rises to 408m (1340ft). ▶ Turn right to reach a bench overlooking Welshpool and the hills beyond. Walk round the ditch to the far side of the embankment.

Head downhill as marked, parallel to a track, later joining and following the track further downhill. When the track suddenly turns left, keep straight ahead downhill. Walk along the inside edge of a forest, then leave it and turn right downhill beside it. Go through a gate and continue straight down a narrow road to a junction at **Pant-y-bwch**.

Turn left as signposted and follow the road round a bend, then turn right down a woodland path. Pass a pond with a dam and keep left to follow a track through forest. This rises gently, then keep right to cross two stone-built bridges above an old brick-built dam. Watch out on the left for wooden steps climbing up the forested slope as signposted. The well-forested path follows the embankment and ditch of **Offa's Dyke**, later crossing it at its highest point, at almost 300m (985ft), before continuing along and down a track. Turn left at a track junction, then later fork right at another track junction. Follow the track downhill, steepening, to reach a stone-built cottage, then pass a cattle grid to reach a minor road.

Turn right, steeply downhill, noting that the road follows both the course of Offa's Dyke and a Roman road.

Seen from the air, the trees spell out 'EııR' and were planted in the coronation year of 1953. There is a plan to fell the trees and restore grassland to the hill fort.

Woodland inside the hill fort of Beacon Ring, where the trees spell out a hidden message

The road levels out and finally bends right as it reaches the first buildings at the village of **Forden**. Step left onto an access track and immediately turn right to follow a field path. Continue along another field path, then down a muddy path among trees, to reach a track and road junction. Turn left along the road, then quickly right as signposted. Go through a succession of small fields, following a grassy mound, and eventually reach the **A490** road at a house. Turn right along the road and quickly reach a busy road junction. ◄

Turn right up the A490 to Forden for Heath Cottage B&B.

Turn left as signposted for Montgomery along the **B4388**. Follow the cycleway beside the road, crossing to the other side, then later turn left up the farm access road for **Nantcribba**. Turn right before reaching the first house, which is Dol y Maen. Walk through a field, then there are gates either side of a road fork, which is crossed. Follow the embankment and ditch of Offa's Dyke past stout oaks, then continue practically in a straight line down through fields, passing stiles and gates, crossing a farm access road in a dip near another part of the village of **Forden**.

Trees and a linear mound reveal the course of Offa's Dyke in fields

Cross gently rolling hills, with trees alongside the Dyke, then cross to the other side in a muddy dip, where

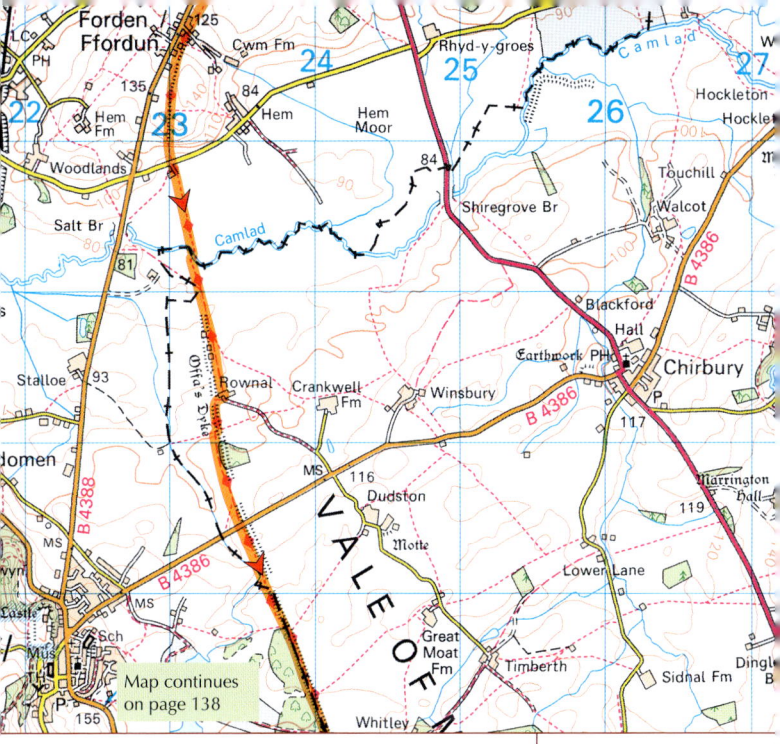

there is a duckboard. Soon afterwards, drop steeply downhill through the 'Bloodiest Battlefield'. ▶ Continue down through a gate, cross a footbridge and reach a gate onto a road. Cross the road and continue along a track, passing Pound House.

An obvious grassy track passes between fields, but watch for a little footbridge with gates on the right. Cross it and turn left. Later, cross a bigger footbridge with gates over the **Camlad** and pass into Shropshire at this point. Cross a little bridge over a stream and follow a grassy path, enclosed by fences and overgrown hedgerows. Pass a couple of boarded-up buildings then climb beside a field to the farm of **Rownal**.

Turn right along a track, away from the farm, then left up through a small gate. Follow a path beside the embankment of Offa's Dyke, which has trees along the

A notice explains about a Civil War clash here on 18 Sept 1644.

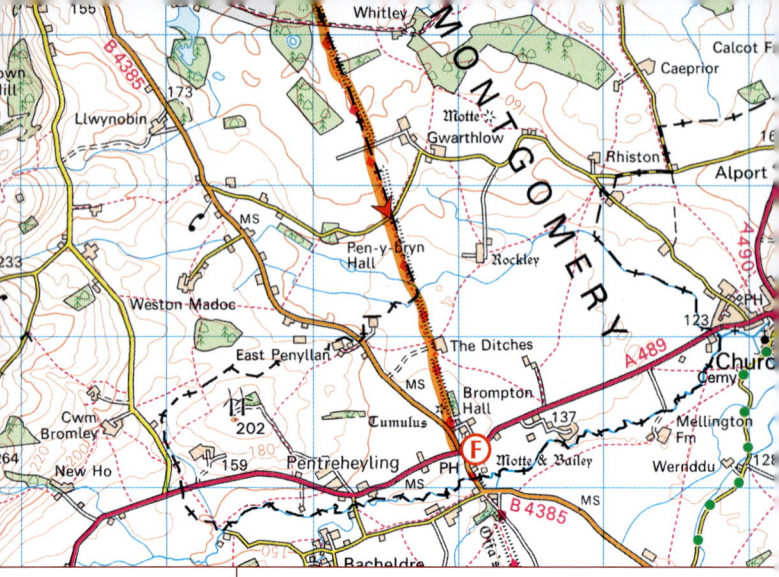

Go right (off-route) to follow the B4386 to Montgomery, which offers a post office, shops, pub, café, accommodation, museum and bus services to Welshpool and Shrewsbury. Montgomery Castle ruins rise above the town.

The crossroads is entirely in England, but – rather oddly – all four roads quickly lead into Wales!

top. Turn right and left to cross the Dyke and continue along the other side. A track undulates and eventually reaches the **B4386** road. ◂ Cross a stile and follow a clear embankment at first, with stout oak trees along it. The line of Offa's Dyke marks the boundary between England, to the left, and Wales, to the right. Simply walk straight ahead through fields as marked, linking stiles and gates. The Dyke is less well defined, but usually bears trees and bushes.

Cross a narrow farm access road at a cattle grid near **Whitley**, and at the same time switch from the English to Welsh side of the Dyke. Continue straight ahead through fields as signposted and marked. Some stretches of the ditch alongside contain water. Cross a minor road near **Pen-y-bryn** and continue as marked through fields. Pass a house called **The Ditches** and continue straight through the farmyard to reach fields beyond, and eventually reach **Brompton Hall**. Turn right along its access track, then left along the B4385 to reach a crossroads and the Blue Bell Hotel at **Brompton Cross**. ◂ Occasional buses run daily, except Sundays, to Church Stoke, Montgomery, Welshpool and Newtown.

DAY 11
Brompton Cross to Knighton

Start	Blue Bell Hotel, Brompton Cross
Finish	Clock Tower, Knighton
Distance	24.5km (15¼ miles)
Ascent	1020m (3345ft)
Descent	975m (3200ft)
Time	8hr
Terrain	Low-lying farmland, then a succession of ascents and descents over hills and valleys, steep at times, with wooded and open areas
Maps	OS Landranger 137
Refreshment	Blue Bell Hotel at Brompton Cross. Bar restaurant off-route at Mellington Hall. Crown Inn off-route at Newcastle. Plenty of choice in Knighton.
Transport	Buses link Montgomery with Forden, Welshpool, Oswestry and Shrewsbury. Knighton is served by trains from Shrewsbury and Swansea. Buses link Knighton with Kington and Newtown.

This stretch of Offa's Dyke Path involves more ascent than any part of Glyndŵr's Way. Although the overall altitude is never particularly great, the frequency and steepness of the slopes makes for slow progress on a few occasions. If this stretch proves too arduous, it can be broken at the village of Newcastle. Not only does the path stay very close to Offa's Dyke, but the Dyke itself is particularly tall and stout throughout this region and is referred to as the High Dyke. It can often be seen in view ahead, snaking across the countryside, apparently with little regard to the shape of the landscape.

Leave the Blue Bell Hotel at **Brompton Cross**, around 140m (460ft), and follow the road signposted for Mellington. Watch out on the left for a hill-like motte and bailey, as well as Brompton Mill. Cross a bridge

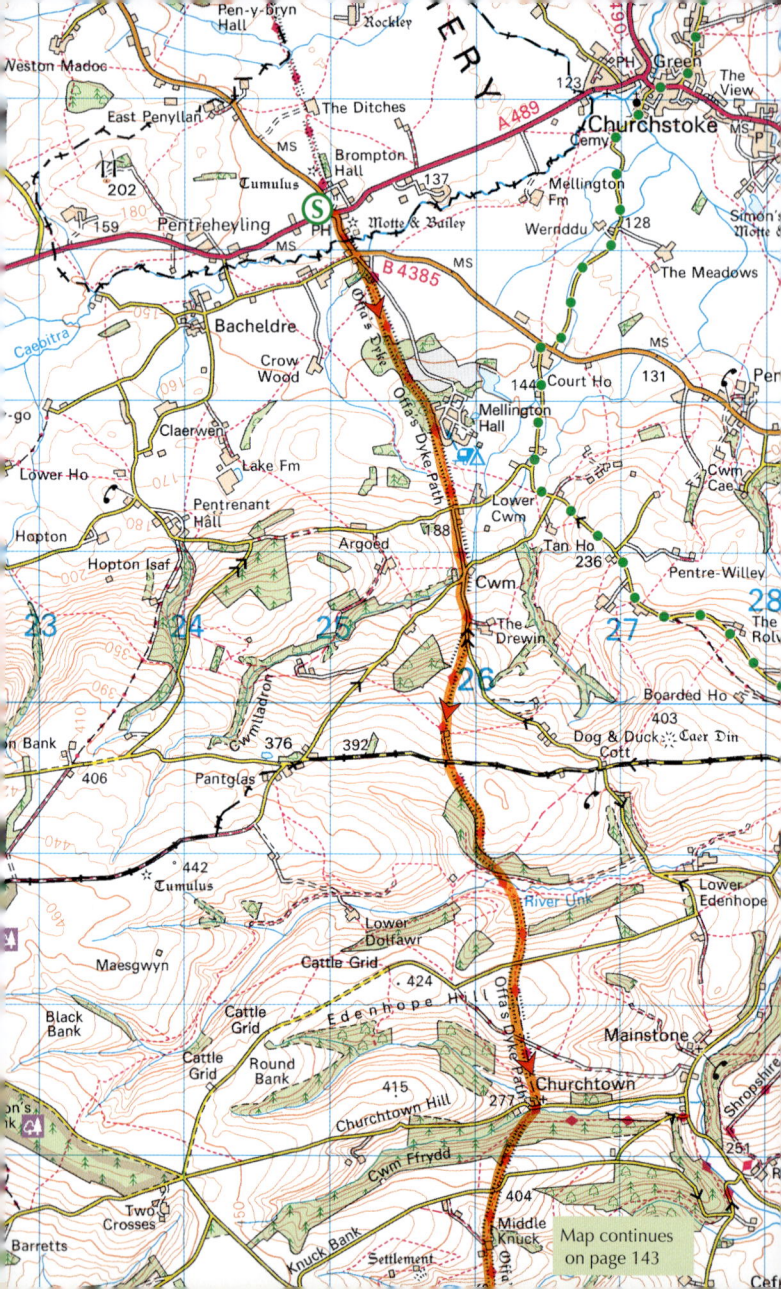

DAY 11 – BROMPTON CROSS TO KNIGHTON

over a river to enter Powys, then go through an imposing gatehouse arch, remembering to shut the iron gate. Walk along a narrow tree-lined road, then as soon as a road bend is reached, turn right along a woodland path, which quickly bends left. Leave the wood to walk alongside a field, then head back into the woods, noting regularly spaced lime trees on top of the Dyke. The path climbs, then crosses a woodland track near **Mellington Hall**. ▶

Turn left to reach the hall, an imposing building, which offers food, drink and accommodation, with a campsite in the grounds.

The Dyke, which is well wooded, passes mobile homes near Mellington Hall and later crosses a farm track. Climb, passing through a small gate to reach a road junction. Continue straight ahead, passing the Offa's Dyke Cottage B&B, walking downhill and uphill. Pass a road junction at **Cwm** and fork left uphill as signposted for Mainstone. Climb past an access road for **Drewin**. The road climbs more steeply, then a signpost points right over a stile into a field. Walk on top of the earthwork, with trees on either side. The Dyke then becomes a field boundary, rising past a house called Nyth Bran or Crowsnest. Follow its access track uphill and cross a road on the Kerry Ridgeway, around 380m (1245ft). ▶

The Kerry Ridgeway has a long history and is sometimes called the 'Oldest Road in Wales'.

Go through a gate welcoming walkers to Shropshire. Walk to another gate nearby, turning quickly left and right, then walk beside the Dyke. Later, the earthwork runs beside a forest and drops steeply into a valley. Cross a footbridge over the **River Unk**, around 300m

Walkers on top of Offa's Dyke high above Mellington

(985ft), then follow the earthwork uphill. Climb steeply as signposted and marked, crossing a minor road on **Edenhope Hill**. Walk along the top of the Dyke, crossing a stile on top of the hill, over 415m (1360ft). Keep walking along the top of the Dyke, gently downhill at first, then more steeply. Cross a track and drop even more steeply, with more trees alongside, to reach the bottom of a valley at **Churchtown**, around 250m (820ft). Go through a gate and cross a minor road, with a little church just to the left.

Cross a footbridge, then walk up a path and wooden steps, through a gate into a forest. Keep straight ahead uphill as signposted. The slope is well wooded, but the trees thin out, and a field path leads to gates and a road crossing at Knuck, at 404m (1325ft). The Dyke and path continue, then drop steeply, with larches planted along the embankment. Cross a little footbridge and follow the path to cross a road at **Middle Knuck**. Go up through a small gate and turn left beside a field. Enter the next field and drop more and more steeply, crossing a footbridge at the bottom at Eaton's Coppice.

Climb steeply past stout sycamores, cross a stile and climb wooden steps, then walk up through the next field at a gentler gradient. Walk through the field beyond, gently up and down, then down through the next field. Cross a stile halfway down into yet another field and continue down into a dip. Walk uphill a little and turn right, as marked, through a gap in the Dyke. Reach a minor road bend below the grassy hill of **Hergan**, around 360m (1180ft).

Cross the road and go through a gate, then walk down a broad grassy path to pass a water tank. Be sure to keep heading gently downhill and not to follow any paths uphill. Hawthorn trees rise alongside the embankment and ditch. A short path rises to cross a stile in a hedge and fence, then a grassy path runs downhill. This steepens, then a long flight of wooden steps drops down a wooded slope to a stile. Cross a dip in a field, rise a short way, then follow the path down across a wooded slope. Go through a gate and pass a house at the foot of **Mount**

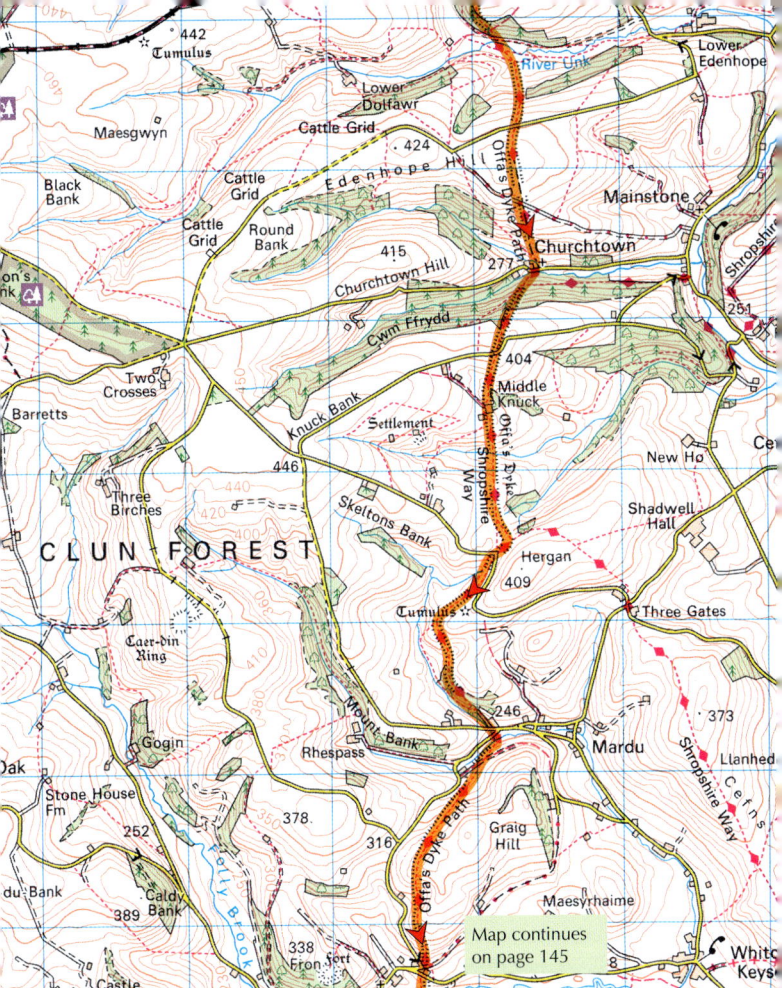

Bank. Turn left and right at road junctions close together, around 250m (820ft).

Turn left to go through a small gate and cross a footbridge. The path climbs through fields and reaches a track junction above a farm. Follow the grassy track uphill, and as it climbs, notice that it runs roughly parallel to a minor

A farm track above Lower Spoad, which runs beside the tall embankment of Offa's Dyke

It is 88½ miles, south and north, to the start and finish of the Offa's Dyke Path.

The nearest accommodation, Quarry House, is only a few paces away. The village of Newcastle offers pub accommodation at the Crown Inn.

road. Follow the path as marked from field to field across the hillside. Cross a track and go up a few steps through a kissing gate. Follow the Dyke up to another kissing gate on the shoulder of **Graig Hill**, around 350m (1150ft). Head down the other side, dropping steeply past larches planted on the Dyke. Cross a hollow in the hillside, walk through a gate, then the path climbs a short way. Walk downhill again, through a kissing gate, and pass the Offa's Dyke Path 'Halfway' signpost. ◄ Cross a track and reach a minor road, from where the village of **Newcastle-on-Clun** is 1.2km (¾ mile) off-route to the right. ◄

Cross the road and keep straight ahead as marked, down through a field to cross a footbridge near **Bryndrinog**, spanning the River Clun, around 200m (655ft). Keep to the field edge as requested, then climb through a field to the B4368 road at **Lower Spoad**. Turn left along the road and quickly right through the farmyard. Follow a clear track straight uphill, with a stream to the left. Later, the track bends left, then when a fork is reached, keep right and keep climbing. Later still, keep straight ahead up a grassy track, with the Dyke alongside, and cross a stile beside a gate. The Dyke is low, planted with hawthorn trees as it climbs. A track later continues up to a minor road at **Springhill Farm**, which offers a campsite, around 400m (1310ft).

Turn right along the road, past the farm, then turn left at a crossroads, down the road signposted for Cwm Collo. The road crosses a dip, and rises and falls, with the Dyke running parallel to the left, quite overgrown. Looking ahead, the earthwork can be seen slicing across a grassy hillside, but the road pulls away from it, crosses a stream in a dip, then climbs. Although there is a signpost pointing left towards the Dyke, keep climbing along the road until an Offa's Dyke signpost points left along a grassy track.

Rise gently, then veer left (in effect straight ahead) along a gravel track. This generally rises, flanked by fences, gradually coming closer to the Dyke on the slopes of **Llanfair Hill.** When the track passes through a gate, the Dyke is very close. In fact, the embankment is accompanied by a public footpath and can be followed if desired, but the 'official' route follows the track. Later, the track slices through the Dyke, around 430m (1410ft), and again either course can be followed. Pass a small forest plantation and a corrugated barn, then later the gravel track turns right. Don't follow it, but continue straight ahead, along and gently down a grassy track. Go through gates, following the track through fields, with the Dyke lying far to the right, bearing larch trees. The track suddenly cuts through a gap in the Dyke, then runs down to **Garbett Hall**. Keep left of the buildings and cross a minor road.

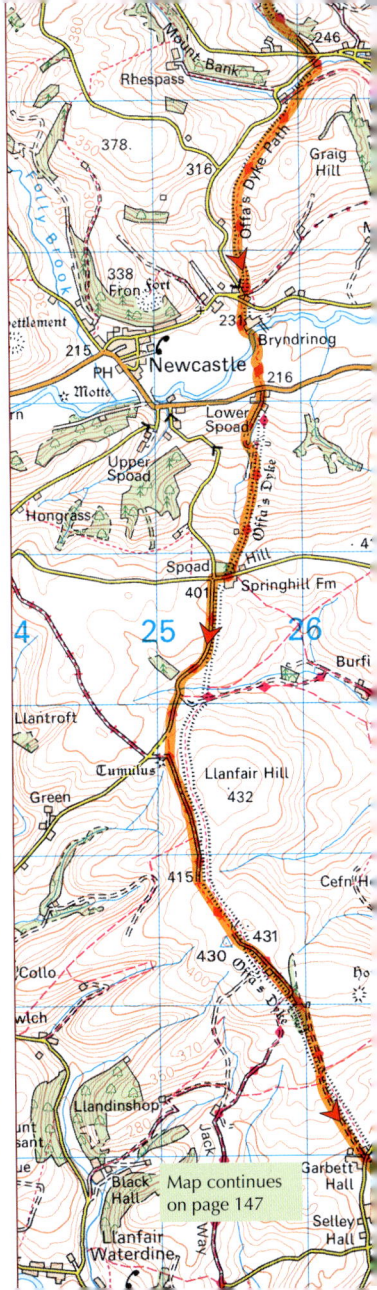

Looking back along a path that climbs steeply from Brynorgan to Cwm-sanaham Hill

Cross a stile and walk down wooden steps, then cross a footbridge over a stream. Climb a little and walk along and down a short stretch of the Dyke among woods. Cross another footbridge and walk up to a track. Cross this and keep climbing, going through a kissing gate, then turn right downhill, reaching a kissing gate, where steps drop to a road near **Selley Hall**, around 260m (855ft).

Turn left up the road, and almost immediately right through a gate, down a track. The track soon climbs and passes the hidden farmhouse of Brynorgan, where it levels out. Go through a gate and climb a steep path. The line of the Dyke is indistinct, but the clearest path accompanies it to the top of the steep slope. Keep straight ahead along a gentler path on a grassy slope. The Dyke is now a low grassy embankment with a fence alongside, and a stile is crossed on the way up to **Cwm-sanaham Hill**, where there is a trig point around 405m (1330ft). Enjoy views, which include a glimpse of Knighton and nearby hilly parts of Shropshire, while across the Teme valley, rolling hills stretch into mid-Wales.

Step down to a marker post and follow a path past Scots pines and larches, and later cross a track at the head of a steep-sided valley. The path rises, then cuts down and up across a slope in front of a forest. Continue following the grassy embankment of the Dyke, dropping into a dip and crossing a track. Continue alongside the

A view of Knighton from Panpunton Hill, with the Clock Tower in the centre of the picture

low embankment, with a building down to the right. Larches have been planted along the Dyke, although these end later, and a fence follows the embankment. The Dyke later crosses a dip below the gentle grassy top of **Panpunton Hill**. Rise, then descend a short way into another dip, then rise to a memorial bench overlooking Knighton, the Teme valley and distant mountains.

The path goes through a gate and heads downhill beside mixed woodland. Cross a track, and shortly afterwards at a signpost, the path turns right and drops steeply. Walk down through a wood, where the path becomes braided, reaching a road beside **Panpunton Farm**. Cross the road and continue down to the **River Teme**. Cross a railway line with care, then cross a footbridge spanning the river, beside a railway bridge. Continue walking downstream, first through a riverside meadow, then through woods. Pass a sign reading 'Welcome to Wales'.

Turn right as marked, up from the woods, then up through a grassy hollow, past fitness equipment. Walk up a road to reach the Offa's Dyke Centre, which doubles as a tourist information centre. Turn left to follow

DAY 11 – BROMPTON CROSS TO KNIGHTON

the main road down into **Knighton**, reaching the Clock Tower in the centre of town, around 185m (610ft). The Offa's Dyke Path continues straight ahead down the road, while Glyndŵr's Way starts on the right, climbing up High Street.

KNIGHTON

The small market town of Knighton, with a charter granted in 1230, is also known as Tref-y-Clawdd ('town on the dyke'). The dyke referred to is the eighth-century Offa's Dyke, which passes straight through the centre of the town, and some of its finest stretches run over nearby hills. There are also the remains of two Norman motte and baileys – one of them marked on the map as Bryn-y-Castell, and the other located at the highest point in town, on private land. The higher castle was destroyed by Owain Glyndŵr in 1402. The bulk of Knighton is in Wales, but a few buildings on the northern side of the River Teme lie in England, making this a true border (or 'Marches') town. Anyone able to spare the time to explore should start at the Offa's Dyke Centre, which provides lots of local information, as well as commentaries about Offa's Dyke, King Offa of Mercia, Owain Glyndŵr and Glyndŵr's Way (tel 01547 528753).

Knighton is served by the Heart of Wales line, which runs between Shrewsbury and Swansea, featuring splendid scenery for the most part. The town offers a fine range of services, including hotels, B&Bs and a nearby campsite, as well as plenty of shops, pubs, restaurants, cafés and take-aways. There is a post office, bank with ATM, local bus services and taxis. The next place with a similar range of services, Llanidloes, is three days ahead along the trail.

APPENDIX A
Facilities along the route

Day	Location (stage start/finish shown in bold)	Distance from day start	Distance from route start	B&B/hotel	Bunkhouse	Campsite	Pub/café	Shop	Cashpoint
1	**Knighton**	0km (0 miles)	0km (0 miles)	Y		Y	Y	Y	Y
	Llangunllo	10km (6¼ miles)	10km (6¼ miles)	Y*			Y		
	Felindre	24.5km (15¼ miles)	24.5km (15¼ miles)	Y	Y	Y	Y	Y*	
2	Llanbadarn Fynydd	11km (7 miles)	35.5km (22¼ miles)					Y	
	Abbeycwmhir	25km (15½ miles)	49.5km (30¾ miles)	Y		Y	Y		
	Bwlch-y-sarnau	5.5km (3½ miles)	55km (34¼ miles)				Y		
3	Newchapel	21.5km (13½ miles)	71km (44¼ miles)			Y			
	Plas Newydd	23.5km (14½ miles)	73km (45¼ miles)		Y				
	Llanidloes	25km (15½ miles)	74.5km (46¼ miles)	Y		Y	Y	Y	Y
4	Llyn Clywedog	10km (6¼ miles)	84.5km (52½ miles)	Y			Y		
	Dolydd	17.5km (11 miles)	92 (57¼miles)						
	Staylittle	19km (12 miles)	93.5km (58¼ miles)	Y*				Y*	

Appendix A – Facilities along the route

Day	Location (stage start/finish shown in bold)	Distance from day start	Distance from route start	B&B/hotel	Bunkhouse	Campsite	Pub/café	Shop	Cashpoint
	Dyfi	22 km (13¾ miles)	96.5km (60 miles)	Y*					
5	Talbontdrain	15km (9½ miles)	111.5km (69½ miles)	Y					
	Machynlleth	25.5km (16 miles)	122km (76 miles)	Y			Y	Y	Y
6	Forge	2km (1¼ miles)	124km (77¼ miles)	Y					
	Penegoes	4km (2½ miles)	126km (78½ miles)	Y*					
	Cemmaes Road	14.5km (9 miles)	136.5km (85 miles)	Y				Y	
	Llanbrynmair	26km (16 miles)	148km (92 miles)	Y		Y*	Y	Y	
7	Llangadfan	19km (12 miles)	167km (104 miles)	Y		Y	Y	Y	
	Ddôl Cownwy	27.5km (17 miles)	175.5km (109 miles)	Y*					
	Llanwddyn	29.5km (18½ miles)	177.5km (110½ miles)	Y			Y		
8	Abertridwr	1.5km (1 mile)	179km (111½ miles)			Y		Y	
	Pont Llogel	6.5km (4 miles)	184km (114½ miles)					Y	
	Dolanog	13.5km (8¼ miles)	191km (118¾ miles)			Y*			

GLYNDŴR'S WAY

Day	Location (stage start/finish shown in bold)	Distance from day start	Distance from route start	B&B/hotel	Bunkhouse	Campsite	Pub/café	Shop	Cashpoint
	Pontrobert	19km (12 miles)	196.5km (122½ miles)				Y		
	Meifod	24.5km (15¼ miles)	202km (125¾ miles)	Y		Y*	Y	Y	
9	**Welshpool**	18km (11 miles)	220km (136¾ miles)	Y	Y*	Y*	Y	Y	Y
10	Buttington	3km (2 miles)	223km (138¾ miles)			Y	Y	Y	
	Forden	13km (8 miles)	233km (144¾ miles)	Y					
	Montgomery	18km (11 miles)	238km (147¾ miles)	Y*			Y*	Y*	Y*
	Brompton Cross	22.5km (14 miles)	242.5km (150¾ miles)				Y		
11	Mellington Hall	1.5km (1 mile)	244km (151¾ miles)	Y		Y	Y		
	Newcastle	12km (7½ miles)	254.5km (158¼ miles)	Y*			Y*		
	Springhill	13.5km (8½ miles)	256km (159¼ miles)			Y			
	Knighton	24.5km (15¼ miles)	267km (166 miles)	Y		Y	Y	Y	Y

* off-route only

APPENDIX B
Pronunciation guide and topographical glossary

Pronunciation should be easy once you learn the 'rules', as Welsh is largely phonetic. Although some vowels and consonants sound the same as in English, others are different. One or two sounds have no close English equivalent, and are best learned by listening carefully to a native speaker. Vowels, which also include 'w' and 'y', have long or short forms, depending on whether they have a circumflex, known in Welsh as a 'to bach'.

Place-name elements often appear on maps, and it is interesting to try and translate names while passing through the countryside. In some instances place names describe particular landforms perfectly, while in other instances they describe what the landscape might once have looked like, before places and even whole areas were drastically altered.

a/â	short form as in 'c**a**t' and long form as in '**aa**h'	ll	no English equivalent, so pronounce it as '**thl**' until you are able to hear and copy the sound correctly
ae/ai/au	as English '**eye**'		
aw	as English 'h**ow**'	m	as English '**m**ore'
b	as English '**b**est'	n	as English '**n**one'
c	as English '**c**at', always hard and never soft	ng	as English 'fi**ng**er'
ch	as in the guttural Scottish sound at the end of 'lo**ch**'	o/ô	short form as in 'h**o**t' and long form as in 'f**oe**'
d	as English '**d**ig'	oe/oi	as English 'b**oy**'
dd	as English '**th**' in '**th**is' and '**th**at'	p	as English '**p**ick'
e/ê	short form as in 'g**e**t' and long form as in 'g**a**te'	r	as English '**r**ip' and sometimes slightly rolled
eu/ei	as English 'h**ay**'	rh	pronounced '**hr**' as if the letters are reversed
ew	no English equivalent, so pronounce it somewhere between '**eh-oo**' and '**ow-oo**'	s	as English '**s**ip'
		si	as English '**sh**ip'
		t	as English '**t**ip'
f	as English '**v**ary'	th	as English '**th**ank' or '**th**ink'
ff	as English '**f**ish'	u/û	short form as in 'p**i**t' and long form as '**ee**'
g	as English '**g**ot', always hard and never soft	w/ŵ	short form as in 'h**oo**t' or 'p**u**p' and long form as a longer '**oo**'. However, it can also be pronounced the English way, as in '**w**in', in certain words.
h	as English 'h**o**t', always pronounced and never silent		
i/î	short form as in 'p**i**n' and long form as in 's**ee**n'		
iw	as English 'y**ew**'	wy	as English '**w**in'
l	as English '**l**ook'	y/ŷ	short form varies from a short '**ee**' to '**uh**' and long form is a longer '**ee**'
		yw	as English 'y**ew**'
		ywy	as English '**oo-ee**'

GLYNDŴR'S WAY

One important point to note is that some names 'mutate' in Welsh, so that 'pont' becomes 'bont', and 'bach' becomes 'fach'. The list therefore includes a lot of repetition.

aber	river mouth	*glas*	blue
afon	river	*gôch/côch*	red
allt	wooded slope	*graig/craig*	rock
bach/fach	small	*gwaun/waun*	marshy moor/meadow
ban/fan	summit	*gwern*	alder
banc	hillock/mound	*gwyn/wen/wyn*	white
bont/pont	bridge	*hafod*	summer farm
bron/fron	slope	*hen*	old
bryn	hill	*isaf*	lower
bwlch	gap/pass	*llan*	church
caer/gaer	fort	*llechwedd*	hillside
carn/garn	cairn	*llwyd/lwyd*	grey
castell	castle	*llyn*	lake
cefn	ridge	*maes*	field
côch/gôch	red	*mawr/fawr*	great
coed	wood	*moel/foel*	bald
craig/graig	rock	*mynydd*	mountain
cwm	valley	*nant*	stream
dinas	fort/citadel	*pant*	hollow
dôl	meadow	*pen*	head/end
dref/tref	town	*pentre*	village
dyffryn	vale	*plas*	hall
eglwys	church	*pont/bont*	bridge
esgair	ridge	*pwll*	pool
fach/bach	small	*rhiw*	hill
fan/ban	summit	*rhos*	moor
fawr/mawr	great	*tref/dref*	town
ffordd	road	*tŷ*	house
ffridd	mountain pasture	*uchaf*	upper
foel/moel	bald	*waun/gwaun*	marshy moor/meadow
fron/bron	slope	*y/yr*	the
gaer/caer	fort		
garn/carn	cairn		
glan	riverbank		

APPENDIX C
Useful contacts

Glyndŵr's Way National Trail
The official Glyndŵr's Way National Trail website is available in English and Welsh, and contains a wealth of useful information. In particular, there are full details of all the available accommodation, including campsites and bunkhouses, as well as shops, pubs, restaurants, cafés and everything else that walkers might like to know about in advance. If walkers experience any problems with Glyndŵr's Way, and in particular with its signposts, waymarks and general infrastructure, contact the Trail Officer. See www.nationaltrail.co.uk/en_GB/trails/glyndwrs-way.

Offa's Dyke Path
For information on the Offa's Dyke Path see www.nationaltrail.co.uk/en_GB/trails/offas-dyke-path.

Powys County Council
The whole of Glyndŵr's Way is confined within the county of Powys. The County Council website is available in English and Welsh, and has plenty of information about council services. See www.powys.gov.uk.

Glyndŵr's Way is marked with both the standard National Trail acorn logo, as well as a distinctive dragon logo

GLYNDŴR'S WAY

Tourism

For general tourism topics, see
www.midwalesmyway.com

Offa's Dyke Centre
Knighton
tel 01547 528753

Tourist Information Centre
Welshpool
tel 01938 552043

Public transport

Trains

There are two railway lines through mid-Wales – the Cambrian Line and the Heart of Wales Line. Trains on both lines are operated by Transport for Wales. Three of the four towns on Glyndŵr's Way have railway stations – Knighton, Machynlleth and Welshpool – along with the village of Llangunllo. Full details of train services, timetables and ticket prices can be checked on tfw.wales.

Buses

While there are a few regular bus services linking a small number of towns and villages along Glyndŵr's Way, there are also long stretches of the route that have no bus services at all. Full details of all available buses and trains are best checked on Traveline-Cymru www.traveline.cymru.

Walking holidays/baggage transfer

Byways Breaks
0151 722 8050
www.byways-breaks.co.uk

Celtic Trails
tel 01291 689774
www.celtictrailswalkingholidays.co.uk

Contours Walking Holidays
tel 01629 821900
www.contours.co.uk

Wildlife and bird watching

Radnorshire Wildlife Trust
www.rwtwales.org

Montgomery Wildlife Trust
www.montwt.co.uk

Dyfi Osprey Project
www.dyfiospreyproject.com

RSPB
www.rspb.org.uk

APPENDIX D
Accommodation along the route

Information given here was correct at the time of going to press but is naturally subject to change. Please check ahead before relying on any establishment listed still offering accommodation.

Location	Name	Postcode	Telephone	Distance off-route
Knighton	George & Dragon Inn, Broad Street	LD7 1BL	01547 528532	
	The Knighton Hotel, Broad Street	LD7 1BL	01547 520530	
	Horse & Jockey, Station Road	LD7 1AE	01547 520062	
	Plough Inn, Market Street	LD7 1EY	01547 528041	
	Red Lion, West Street	LD7 1EN	01547 428080	
	Beech Villa, West Street	LD7 1EN	07375 320239	
	Whytcwm Cottage, George Road	LD7 1HF	07904 971866	
	The Kinsley, Station Road	LD7 1DT	01547 520753	
	Westwood, Presteigne Road	LD7 1HY	01547 520317	
	Panpwnton Farm, Kinsley Road (Camping)	LD7 1TN	07794 664407	1km (½ mile)
Llangunllo Station	Rhiwlas	LD7 1SY	01547 550256	
Felindre	Brandy House Farm (B&B and Camping Pods)	LD7 1YL	01547 510282	
	Trevland (B&B, Bunkhouse and Camping)	LD7 1YL	01547 510211	
AAbbeycwmhir	Laurel Bank	LD1 6PH	01597 851240	

GLYNDŴR'S WAY

Location	Name	Postcode	Telephone	Distance off-route
	Home Farm (Camping)	LD1 6PH	01597 851666	
	The Oaks	LD1 6PH	07967 298725	
Newchapel	Cwm Farm (Camping)	SY18 6LH	01686 413544	
Before Llanidloes	Plas Newydd, Gorn Road (Bunkhouse)	SY18 6LA	01686 412431	
Llanidloes	Idloes House, Shortbridge Street	S18 6AD	01686 413821	
	The Trewythen, Great Oak Street	SY18 6BW	01686 411333	
	Mount Inn, China Street	SY18 6AB	01686 412247	
	Coach and Horses, Smithfield Street	SY18 6EJ	01686 413758	
	Red Lion Hotel, Longbridge Street	SY18 6EE	01686 412270	
	Unicorn Hotel, Longbridge Street	SY18 6BW	01686 411188	
	Dol Llys Farm (Camping)	SY18 6JA	01686 412694	1km (½ mile)
Llyn Clywedog	Ty Capel B&B	SY18 6NX	07484 143877	
Dolydd	Hafren Forest Bunkhouse	SY19 7DB	07871 740514	
Staylittle	The Lodge	SY19 7BU	07790 761859	1.5km (1 mile)
Dylife	Y Star Inn	SY19 7BW	01650 521434	1km (½ mile)
Pennant	The Old School House B&B	SY19 7BL	01650 521486	6.5km (4 miles)

Appendix D – Accommodation along the route

Location	Name	Postcode	Telephone	Distance off-route
Talbontdrain	Talbontdrain	SY20 8RR	07972 584915	
Machynlleth	Wynnstay Hotel, Heol Maengwyn	SY20 8AE	01654 702941	
	White Lion Hotel, Heol Pentrehedyn	SY20 8DN	01654 703455	
	Maenllwyd, Newtown Road	SY20 8EY	01654 702928	
	Toad Hall Hostel, Railway Terrace	SY20 8BH	07866 362507	
Forge	Cwm Dylluan	SY20 8RZ	01654 702684	
Penegoes	Llwyn (B&B and Camping)	SY20 8NH	01654 703733	
Cemmaes Road	Moelfre B&B	SY20 8LF	07498 720679	
	Dovey Valley Hotel	SY20 8JZ	01650 511335	
Llanbrynmair	Wynnstay Arms Hotel	SY19 7AA	01650 521431	
	Wynnstay House	SY19 7DJ	01650 521201	
	Cringoed, Llan (Camping)	SY19 7DR	01650 521237	2km (1¼ miles)
Llangadfan	Cann Office Hotel	SY21 0PL	01938 820202	
	Riverbend Caravan Park (Camping)	SY21 0PP	01938 820356	
Ddôl Cownwy	Hill Farm, Penisarcwm	SY10 0NJ	01691 870655	1km (½ mile)
Llanwddyn	Dam View Cottage	SY10 0LZ	07400 229982	

GLYNDŴR'S WAY

Location	Name	Postcode	Telephone	Distance off-route
Abertridwr	Lake Vyrnwy Hotel	SY10 0LY	01691 870692	1.5km (1 mile)
	Lake Vyrnwy Campsite	SY10 0LS	none	1km (½ mile)
Dolanog	Camp Plas, Plas Dolanog	SY21 0NA	none	1km (½ mile)
Meifod	Kings Head Hotel (and Camping)	SY22 6BY	01938 500867	
	Tan y Graig	SY22 6BP	01938 500574	2.5km (1½ miles)
	Pentrego Farm (Camping)	SY22 6DH	01938 500353	
Welshpool	The Stone House, Mount Street	SK21 7LJ	01938 691039	
	Royal Oak Hotel, The Cross	SY21 7DD	01938 552217	
	Westwood Park Hotel, Salop Road	SY21 7EA	01938 553474	
	Severn Farm, Severn Lane (Camping)	SY21 7BB	01938 555999	
Buttington	Green Dragon Inn (Camping)	SY21 8SS	01938 553076	
Forden	Heath Cottage	SY21 8LX	01938 580453	
	Edderton Hall	SY21 8RZ	01938 580339	2km (1¼ miles)
	Railway Inn	SY21 8NN	01938 580661	1.5km (1 mile)
Montgomery	Dragon Hotel, Market Square	SY15 6PA	01686 668359	2km (1¼ miles)
	The Old Stores	SY15 6RA	07939 378844	2km (1¼ miles)

Appendix D – Accommodation along the route

Location	Name	Postcode	Telephone	Distance off-route
	The Checkers, Broad Street	SY15 6PN	01686 639548	2km (1¼ miles)
Mellington	Mellington Hall	SY15 6HX	01588 620056	
	Mellington Hall Holiday Home Park (Camping)	SY15 6HX	01588 620011	
Lower Cwm	Offa's Dyke Cottage	SY15 6TH	01588 620642	
Newcastle	Quarry House, Church Road	SY7 8QJ	01588 640774	
	Crown Inn	SY7 8QL	01588 640271	1km (¼ mile)
	Little Hall Cottage	SY7 8PA	01588 640976	1.5km (1 mile)
Spoad Hill	Springhill Farm (Camping)	SY7 8PE	01588 640337	
Knighton	George & Dragon Inn, Broad Street	LD7 1BL	01547 528532	
	The Knighton Hotel, Broad Street	LD7 1BL	01547 520530	
	Horse & Jockey, Station Road	LD7 1AE	01547 520062	
	Plough Inn, Market Street	LD7 1EY	01547 528041	
	Red Lion, West Street	LD7 1EN	01547 428080	
	Beech Villa, West Street	LD7 1EN	07375 320239	
	Whytcwm Cottage, George Road	LD7 1HF	07904 971866	
	The Kinsley, Station Road	LD7 1DT	01547 520753	
	Westwood, Presteigne Road	LD7 1HY	01547 520317	
	Panpwnton Farm, Kinsley Road (Camping)	LD7 1TN	07794 664407	1km (½ mile)

NOTES

NOTES

DOWNLOAD THE ROUTES IN GPX FORMAT

All the routes in this guide are available for download from:

www.cicerone.co.uk/1129/GPX

as standard format GPX files. You should be able to load them into most online GPX systems and mobile devices, whether GPS or smartphone. You may need to convert the file into your preferred format using a conversion programme such as gpsvisualizer.com or one of the many other such websites and programmes.

When you follow this link, you will be asked for your email address and where you purchased the guidebook, and have the option to subscribe to the Cicerone e-newsletter.

www.cicerone.co.uk

LISTING OF CICERONE GUIDES

BRITISH ISLES CHALLENGES, COLLECTIONS AND ACTIVITIES

Cycling Land's End to John o' Groats
Great Walks on the England Coast Path
The Big Rounds
The Book of the Bivvy
The Book of the Bothy
The Mountains of England and Wales: Vol 1 Wales
The Mountains of England and Wales: Vol 2 England
The National Trails
Walking the End to End Trail

SHORT WALKS SERIES

Short Walks Hadrian's Wall
Short Walks in Arnside and Silverdale
Short Walks in Cornwall: Falmouth and the Lizard
Short Walks in Dumfries and Galloway
Short Walks in Nidderdale
Short Walks in Pembrokeshire: Tenby and the south
Short Walks in the South Downs: Brighton, Eastbourne and Arundel
Short Walks in the Surrey Hills
Short Walks Lake District – Coniston and Langdale
Short Walks Lake District: Keswick, Borrowdale and Buttermere
Short Walks Lake District: Windermere Ambleside and Grasmere
Short Walks on the Malvern Hills
Short Walks Winchester

SCOTLAND

Ben Nevis and Glen Coe
Cycling in the Hebrides
Cycling the North Coast 500
Great Mountain Days in Scotland
Mountain Biking in Southern and Central Scotland
Mountain Biking in West and North West Scotland
Not the West Highland Way Scotland
Scotland's Best Small Mountains
Scotland's Mountain Ridges
Scottish Wild Country Backpacking
Skye's Cuillin Ridge Traverse
The Borders Abbeys Way
The Great Glen Way
The Great Glen Way Map Booklet
The Hebridean Way
The Hebrides
The Isle of Mull
The Isle of Skye
The Skye Trail
The Southern Upland Way
The West Highland Way
The West Highland Way Map Booklet
Walking Ben Lawers, Rannoch and Atholl
Walking in the Cairngorms
Walking in the Pentland Hills
Walking in the Scottish Borders
Walking in the Southern Uplands
Walking in Torridon, Fisherfield, Fannichs and An Teallach
Walking Loch Lomond and the Trossachs
Walking on Arran
Walking on Harris and Lewis
Walking on Jura, Islay and Colonsay
Walking on Rum and the Small Isles
Walking on the Orkney and Shetland Isles
Walking on Uist and Barra
Walking the Cape Wrath Trail
Walking the Corbetts
  Vol 1 South of the Great Glen
  Vol 2 North of the Great Glen
Walking the Galloway Hills
Walking the John o' Groats Trail
Walking the Munros
  Vol 1 – Southern, Central and Western Highlands
  Vol 2 – Northern Highlands and the Cairngorms
Winter Climbs in the Cairngorms
Winter Climbs: Ben Nevis and Glen Coe

NORTHERN ENGLAND ROUTES

Cycling the Reivers Route
Cycling the Way of the Roses
Hadrian's Cycleway
Hadrian's Wall Path
Hadrian's Wall Path Map Booklet
The Coast to Coast Cycle Route
The Coast to Coast Walk
The Coast to Coast Walk Map Booklet
The Pennine Way
The Pennine Way Map Booklet
Walking the Dales Way
Walking the Dales Way Map Booklet

NORTH-EAST ENGLAND, YORKSHIRE DALES AND PENNINES

Cycling in the Yorkshire Dales
Great Mountain Days in the Pennines
Mountain Biking in the Yorkshire Dales
The Cleveland Way and the Yorkshire Wolds Way
The North York Moors
Trail and Fell Running in the Yorkshire Dales
Walking in County Durham
Walking in Northumberland
Walking in the North Pennines
Walking in the Yorkshire Dales:
  North and East
  South and West
Walking St Cuthbert's Way
Walking St Oswald's Way and Northumberland Coast Path

NORTH-WEST ENGLAND AND THE ISLE OF MAN

Cycling the Pennine Bridleway
Isle of Man Coastal Path
The Lancashire Cycleway
The Lune Valley and Howgills
Walking in Cumbria's Eden Valley
Walking in Lancashire
Walking in the Forest of Bowland and Pendle
Walking on the Isle of Man
Walking on the West Pennine Moors
Walking the Ribble Way
Walks in Silverdale and Arnside

LAKE DISTRICT

Bikepacking in the Lake District
Cycling in the Lake District
Great Mountain Days in the Lake District
Joss Naylor's Lakes, Meres and Waters of the Lake District
Lake District Winter Climbs
Lake District:
  High Level and Fell Walks
  Low Level and Lake Walks
Mountain Biking in the Lake District
Outdoor Adventures with Children – Lake District
Scrambles in the Lake District
  – North
  South
Trail and Fell Running in the Lake District
Walking The Cumbria Way
Walking the Lake District Fells –
  Borrowdale
  Buttermere
  Coniston
  Keswick
  Langdale
  Mardale and the Far East
  Patterdale
  Wasdale
Walking the Tour of the Lake District

DERBYSHIRE, PEAK DISTRICT AND MIDLANDS

Cycling in the Peak District
Dark Peak Walks
Scrambles in the Dark Peak
Walking in Derbyshire
Walking in the Peak District –
  White Peak East
  White Peak West

SOUTHERN ENGLAND

20 Classic Sportive Rides in
  South East England
  South West England
Cycling in the Cotswolds
Mountain Biking on the
  North Downs
  South Downs
Suffolk Coast and Heath Walks
The Cotswold Way
The Cotswold Way Map Booklet
The Kennet and Avon Canal
The Lea Valley Walk
The North Downs Way
The North Downs Way Map Booklet
The Peddars Way and Norfolk Coast Path
The Pilgrims' Way
The Ridgeway National Trail
The Ridgeway National Trail Map Booklet
The South Downs Way
The South Downs Way Map Booklet
The Thames Path
The Thames Path Map Booklet
The Two Moors Way
The Two Moors Way Map Booklet
Walking Hampshire's Test Way
Walking in Cornwall
Walking in Essex
Walking in Kent
Walking in London
Walking in Norfolk
Walking in the Chilterns
Walking in the Cotswolds
Walking in the Isles of Scilly
Walking in the New Forest
Walking in the North Wessex Downs
Walking on Dartmoor
Walking on Guernsey
Walking on Jersey
Walking on the Isle of Wight
Walking the Dartmoor Way
Walking the Jurassic Coast
Walking the South West Coast Path
Walking the South West Coast Path Map Booklets
  – Vol 1: Minehead to St Ives
  – Vol 2: St Ives to Plymouth
  – Vol 3: Plymouth to Poole
Walks in the South Downs National Park

WALES AND WELSH BORDERS

Cycle Touring in Wales
Cycling Lon Las Cymru
Great Mountain Days in Snowdonia
Hillwalking in Shropshire
Mountain Walking in Snowdonia
Offa's Dyke Path
Offa's Dyke Path Map Booklet
Ridges of Snowdonia
Scrambles in Snowdonia
Snowdonia: 30 Low-level and Easy Walks
  – North
  – South
The Cambrian Way
The Pembrokeshire Coast Path
The Pembrokeshire Coast Path Map Booklet
The Snowdonia Way
Walking Glyndwr's Way
Walking in Carmarthenshire
Walking in Pembrokeshire
Walking in the Brecon Beacons
Walking in the Forest of Dean
Walking in the Wye Valley
Walking on Gower
Walking the Severn Way
Walking the Shropshire Way
Walking the Wales Coast Path

INTERNATIONAL CHALLENGES, COLLECTIONS AND ACTIVITIES

Europe's High Points
Walking the Via Francigena Pilgrim Route – Part 1

AFRICA

Kilimanjaro
Walking in the Drakensberg
Walks and Scrambles in the Moroccan Anti-Atlas

ALPS CROSS-BORDER ROUTES

100 Hut Walks in the Alps
Alpine Ski Mountaineering Vol 1 – Western Alps
The Karnischer Hohenweg
The Tour of the Bernina
Trail Running – Chamonix and the Mont Blanc region
Trekking Chamonix to Zermatt
Trekking in the Alps
Trekking in the Silvretta and Ratikon Alps
Trekking Munich to Venice
Trekking the Tour du Mont Blanc
Trekking the Tour du Mont Blanc Map Booklet
Walking in the Alps

PYRENEES AND FRANCE/SPAIN CROSS-BORDER ROUTES

Shorter Treks in the Pyrenees
The Pyrenean Haute Route
The Pyrenees
Trekking the GR11 Trail
Walks and Climbs in the Pyrenees

AUSTRIA

Innsbruck Mountain Adventures
Trekking Austria's Adlerweg
Trekking in Austria's Hohe Tauern
Trekking in Austria's Zillertal Alps
Trekking in the Stubai Alps
Walking in Austria
Walking in the Salzkammergut: the Austrian Lake District

EASTERN EUROPE

The Danube Cycleway Vol 2
The High Tatras
The Mountains of Romania
Walking in Hungary

FRANCE, BELGIUM AND LUXEMBOURG

Camino de Santiago – Via Podiensis
Chamonix Mountain Adventures
Cycle Touring in France
Cycling London to Paris
Cycling the Canal de la Garonne
Cycling the Canal du Midi
Cycling the Route des Grandes Alpes
Mont Blanc Walks
Mountain Adventures in the Maurienne
Short Treks on Corsica
The Elbe Cycle Route
The GR5 Trail
The GR5 Trail – Benelux and Lorraine
The GR5 Trail – Vosges and Jura
The Grand Traverse of the Massif Central
The Moselle Cycle Route
The River Loire Cycle Route
The River Rhone Cycle Route
Trekking in the Vanoise
Trekking the Cathar Way
Trekking the GR10
Trekking the GR20 Corsica
Trekking the Robert Louis Stevenson Trail
Via Ferratas of the French Alps
Walking in Provence – East
Walking in Provence – West
Walking in the Ardennes
Walking in the Auvergne
Walking in the Briançonnais
Walking in the Dordogne
Walking in the Haute Savoie: North
Walking in the Haute Savoie: South
Walking on Corsica
Walking the Brittany Coast Path

GERMANY

Hiking and Cycling in the Black Forest
The Danube Cycleway Vol 1

The Rhine Cycle Route
The Westweg
Walking in the Bavarian Alps

IRELAND
The Wild Atlantic Way and Western Ireland
Walking the Wicklow Way

ITALY
Alta Via – Trekking in the Dolomites – Vols 1&2
Day Walks in the Dolomites
Italy's Grande Traversata delle Alpi
Italy's Sibillini National Park
Ski Touring and Snowshoeing in the Dolomites
The Way of St Francis
Trekking in the Apennines
Trekking the Giants' Trail: Alta Via 1 through the Italian Pennine Alps
Via Ferratas of the Italian Dolomites – Vols 1&2
Walking in Abruzzo
Walking in Italy's Cinque Terre
Walking in Italy's Stelvio National Park
Walking in Sicily
Walking in the Aosta Valley
Walking in the Dolomites
Walking in Tuscany
Walking in Umbria
Walking Lake Como and Maggiore
Walking Lake Garda and Iseo
Walking on the Amalfi Coast
Walking the Via Francigena Pilgrim Route – Parts 2&3
Walks and Treks in the Maritime Alps

MEDITERRANEAN
The High Mountains of Crete
Trekking in Greece
Walking and Trekking in Zagori
Walking and Trekking on Corfu
Walking in Cyprus
Walking on Malta
Walking on the Greek Islands – the Cyclades

NEW ZEALAND AND AUSTRALIA
Hiking the Overland Track

NORTH AMERICA
Hiking and Cycling the California Missions Trail
The John Muir Trail
The Pacific Crest Trail

SOUTH AMERICA
Aconcagua and the Southern Andes
Hiking and Biking Peru's Inca Trails
Trekking in Torres del Paine

SCANDINAVIA, ICELAND AND GREENLAND
Hiking in Norway – South
Trekking in Greenland – The Arctic Circle Trail
Trekking the Kungsleden
Walking and Trekking in Iceland

SLOVENIA, CROATIA, SERBIA, MONTENEGRO AND ALBANIA
Hiking Slovenia's Juliana Trail
Mountain Biking in Slovenia
The Islands of Croatia
The Julian Alps of Slovenia
The Mountains of Montenegro
The Peaks of the Balkans Trail
The Slovene Mountain Trail
Walking in Slovenia: The Karavanke
Walks and Treks in Croatia

SPAIN AND PORTUGAL
Camino de Santiago: Camino Frances
Coastal Walks in Andalucia
Costa Blanca Mountain Adventures
Cycling the Camino de Santiago
Cycling the Ruta Via de la Plata
Mountain Walking in Mallorca
Mountain Walking in Southern Catalunya
Portugal's Rota Vicentina
Spain's Sendero Historico: The GR1
The Andalucian Coast to Coast Walk
The Camino del Norte and Camino Primitivo
The Camino Ingles and Ruta do Mar
The Camino Portugues
The Mountains Around Nerja
The Mountains of Ronda and Grazalema
The Sierras of Extremadura
Trekking in Mallorca
Trekking in the Canary Islands
Trekking the GR7 in Andalucia
Walking and Trekking in the Sierra Nevada
Walking in Andalucia
Walking in Catalunya – Barcelona
Walking in Catalunya – Girona Pyrenees
Walking in Portugal
Walking in the Algarve
Walking in the Picos de Europa
Walking La Via de la Plata and Camino Sanabres
Walking on Gran Canaria
Walking on La Gomera and El Hierro
Walking on La Palma
Walking on Lanzarote and Fuerteventura
Walking on Madeira
Walking on Tenerife
Walking on the Azores
Walking on the Costa Blanca
Walking the Camino dos Faros

SWITZERLAND
Switzerland's Jura Crest Trail
The Swiss Alps
Tour of the Jungfrau Region
Trekking the Swiss Via Alpina
Walking in the Bernese Oberland – Jungfrau region
Walking in the Engadine – Switzerland
Walking in the Valais
Walking in Ticino
Walking in Zermatt and Saas-Fee

CHINA, JAPAN AND ASIA
Hiking and Trekking in the Japan Alps and Mount Fuji
Hiking in Hong Kong
Japan's Kumano Kodo Pilgrimage
Trekking in Tajikistan

HIMALAYA
Annapurna
8000 metres
Everest: A Trekker's Guide
Trekking in Bhutan
Trekking in Ladakh
Trekking in the Himalaya
Trekking in the Karakoram

MOUNTAIN LITERATURE
A Walk in the Clouds
Abode of the Gods
Fifty Years of Adventure
The Pennine Way – the Path, the People, the Journey
Unjustifiable Risk?
Unjustifiable Risk?

TECHNIQUES
Fastpacking
Geocaching in the UK
Map and Compass
Outdoor Photography
The Mountain Hut Book

MINI GUIDES
Alpine Flowers
Navigation
Pocket First Aid and Wilderness Medicine
Snow

For full information on all our guides, order books and eBooks, visit our website: **www.cicerone.co.uk**.

CICERONE

Trust Cicerone to guide your next adventure, wherever it may be around the world...

Discover guides for hiking, mountain walking, backpacking, trekking, trail running, cycling and mountain biking, ski touring, climbing and scrambling in Britain, Europe and worldwide.

Connect with Cicerone online and find inspiration.

- buy books and ebooks
- articles, advice and trip reports
- podcasts and live events
- GPX files and updates
- regular newsletter

cicerone.co.uk